JESUS WORKS HERE

JESUS WORKS HERE

ROBERT J. TAMASY, EDITOR

BROADMAN
&HOLMAN
PUBLISHERS

Nashville, Tennessee

Published by:
Broadman & Holman Publishers
Nashville, Tennessee

Printed in the United States of America

Design: Steven Boyd

4261-08
0-8054-6108-6

Dewey Decimal Classification: 286.132
Subject Headings:
Christian Life\Businessmen—Religious
Life\Businesswomen—Religious Life
Library of Congress Card Catalog Number: 94-12582

Unless otherwise noted, Scripture quotations are from (NIV) the
Holy Bible, New International Version, copyright © 1973, 1978,
1984 by International Bible Society; (NASB) the New American
Standard Bible, © The Lockman Foundation, 1960, 1962, 1963,
1968, 1971, 1972, 1973, 1975, 1977, used by permission; (KJV) King
James Version; and (NKJV) New King James Version, copyright ©
1979, 1980, 1982, Thomas Nelson, Inc., Publishers; and (TLB) The
Living Bible, copyright © Tyndale House Publishers, Wheaton,
Ill., 1971, used by permission.

Library of Congress Cataloging-in-Publication Data
Jesus works here : leading Christians in business talk about how you
can walk with Christ through stress, change, and other challenges
of the workplace / Robert J. Tamasy, ed.
    p. cm.
Includes bibliographical references.
ISBN 0-8054-6108-6
    1. Businessmen—Religious life. 2. Women in business—Religious
life. 3. Business—Religious aspects—Christianity. 4. Business
ethics.
I. Tamasy, Robert.
BV4596.B8J47 1995
248.8'.8—dc20   94-12582
                                                      CIP

*T*his book is dedicated to the many men and women who every day journey to the intimidating, frightening, and often godless workplace to faithfully "fight the good fight," determined to serve and represent Jesus Christ where He has placed them.

Contents

Part Seven

Goal-Setting: Critical to Success

Part Eight

Taming the Tension: Balancing Work and Family

Part Eleven

Hiring Strategies: Finding the Right Person

Part Twelve

It All Has to Start with Christ

Introduction

Downscaling. Streamlining. High-tech. Paradigms. Mergers. Stress. Teamwork. Margin.

No doubt you have noticed the changing vocabulary of today's business world. "Job security" has become a contradiction in terms. With more work to do and fewer people to do it, "time management" is a joke heard during increasingly rare coffee breaks. "Let's do lunch" has come to mean, "You sit at your desk, I'll sit at mine, and we'll try to spend lunchtime crawling from under the pile of unfinished projects that were due yesterday."

Never have we been busier. Never have we been more stressed out. Never has the old Broadway tune, "Stop the World, I Want to Get Off," sounded more comforting.

In the midst of this turmoil, we yearn for stability, a sense that as the winds of change intensify to hurricane magnitude, there is something solid and steadfast on which we can rely. Good news! The Bible tells us, "Jesus Christ is the same yesterday and today and forever" (Heb. 13:8). It *does* not say, "except in the business world." When everything around us seems to be falling apart, we have the assurance that "since we are receiving a kingdom that cannot be shaken, let us be thankful, and so worship God acceptably with reverence and awe" (Heb. 12:28).

In an earlier book, I wrote, "The chasm between the church sanctuary and the corporate boardroom sometimes appears wider than the Grand Canyon."[1] That "chasm" is more perceived than real, but perceptions have a way of becoming reality—unless they are corrected. For too many of us, "church is church, and business is business—and never the twain shall meet."

I remember, as a young Christian, going to worship Sundays and feeling the excitement of gaining new insights into God's Word. Yet on Monday mornings, upon entering the "real world" of the newspaper business, I failed to understand the connection between my faith and the stresses of headlines, deadlines, and the bottom line. What an amazing revelation to look around the newsroom and realize for the first time, "Jesus works here!"

This isn't to say that standing true to our Christian convictions in today's workplace is easy. In an environment that generally wants nothing to do with God, the challenge of effectively and consistently representing Christ may be more formidable than ever. I have known my share of failure, but living for the Lord is not impossible—as Jesus affirmed in Mark 10:27—and the rewards exceed anything that the world around us can offer.

More than seventy-five years ago, Oswald Chambers wrote, "Today men are asking not so much if Christianity is true, but if it is real. Does it amount to anything in actual life?"[2] In these closing years of the twentieth century, men and women are still asking this question—especially those who, like you and me, spend many hours each week in the stress-filled, turbulent, unpredictable environment we call the business community.

In the pages that follow you will find a wealth of insight and understanding from men and women who not only believe Jesus *can* work in a business setting, but also that He *must*. They write to help you and me discover—or recover—the joy of serving as

Christ's ambassadors in a part of the world that needs to be introduced to Him. They know the deep satisfaction of following the exhortation, "Whatever you do, work at it with all your heart, as working for the Lord, not for men" (Col. 3:23).

Chambers' comment about truth and reality could have been written yesterday. For nearly three decades, "All truth is relative" has rumbled through the halls of academia, and this insidious message has filtered into corporate boardrooms and office cubicles. Not many business people see the quest for truth as an overriding concern, but they are pragmatic. They want something real, something they can cling to—something that works. They may concede that Jesus Christ belongs in the surrealistic realm of the sanctuary, but *does He work in the workplace?*

Today, even with the twenty-first century within shouting distance, I am more convinced than ever that the answer to that question is an unwavering and resounding, "Yes!" *Jesus Works Here!* has been compiled to reaffirm this heartfelt conviction.

More than thirty men and women of various vocations and levels of authority attest through personal experience that biblical principles hold true even in the secularized business environment of the 1990s. They write as eyewitnesses, submitting expert testimony that faith in Jesus Christ relates even to such unspiritual workplace concerns as stress, unemployment and career change, decision making, teamwork, time management, and the everyday clash of business and family demands.

Work is sacred. It was ordained by God from the beginning, before the fall of man. After the fall, it just got tougher, frustrating, exhausting, sometimes even boring. But work pursued with excellence and integrity is still pleasing to God, a way of honoring Him by serving in the unique ways He has equipped us.

Our work often provides the opportunities to proclaim Him to a broken, unredeemed world—through our example, as well as by our words. The business and professional people of today have a deep concern for relevance, for things real, as Chambers wrote. The question of Christianity's truth may seem insignificant to them; what they desire is the fulfillment of felt needs.

How could the teachings of a book two thousand years old, the Bible, possibly relate to the environment of PCs, voice mail, leverage, fax machines, and *USA TODAY?*

That's where you and I come in. When we demonstrate that the God of all eternity has a personal interest in contemporary problems like stress, goal setting, steamrolling change, and family pressures, those around us who don't know Christ are bound to want to hear more about Him.

We can argue the truth of Scripture, but too often we find ourselves answering questions few people are asking. What they want to know is: "How can I know if I'm doing the right thing?" "How can I squeeze thirty hours worth of responsibility into a twenty-four-hour day?" "How can I win at work without losing at home?" "What will I do if I lose my job?"

Frankly, we have a lot of the same questions. Christ has the answers, as the contributing authors of this book can attest. It is my hope that as you read *Jesus Works Here!* God will deepen or rekindle your own resolve to live for Him—and work for Him—twenty-four hours a day, seven days a week. And in the process, He can say, "You will be *my* witnesses in Jerusalem *[where you live and work]*, and in all Judea and Samaria *[your community and region]*, and to the ends of the earth" (Acts 1:18, author's italics).

How should you use this book? You can read it as a devotional, one chapter a day, pondering what the author has to say about God's involvement in the area discussed. You may choose to read it cover to cover, or just a section that is of most pressing concern to you at the moment. You may use it as a ready reference to consult when various issues arise. Or you may pass it along to a friend who also needs help in seeing how faith fits on the job.

It is my hope and prayer that God will use this book as an instrument to show you, more than ever, that when you go to work each day, you will have no doubt that *Jesus Works Here!*

1. Robert J. Tamasy, *The Complete Christian Businessman* (Brentwood, Tenn.: Wolgemuth & Hyatt, 1991).

2. Oswald Chambers, *The Place of Help* (Grand Rapids, Mich.: Discovery House, 1989).

Part One

For my yoke is easy and my burden is light.

—Matthew 11:30

Too Stressed for Success?

You might know this guy: He walks cautiously but quickly into the office building, eyes darting from side to side. He steps into the elevator and leans into a corner so he can watch everyone else. He frequently glances at the digital readout of floors passed as the elevator ascends. He mutters a quiet prayer that the elevator won't become stuck between floors.

In his office, papers are scattered everywhere, all representing work "in progress." He shuffles through multiple to-do lists and tries to remember what life was like before stick-on notes. They litter his work area, their different colors signifying absolutely nothing.

Whenever the phone rings, this fellow utters an anguished, "Yes?" He thinks, *Surely no one else has thought of something else for me to do. I'm already committed through 1999.*

His wife calls to remind him of their son's starring role in the fourth grade play that evening. (This was the day he planned to work late to try and get caught up on some crucial projects.) She also reports her car has been running sluggishly. "Oh, and you did remember to mail the mortgage payment so it won't be late, didn't you?" she asks sweetly.

By mid-morning our friend begins to look like someone who has been serenaded by chalk squealing against a blackboard for eight unrelenting hours.

At 10:30, his boss stops by. "Harry, are you all right? You look terrible. Are you feeling a little stressed out?"

"*Stress?*" he cries. "*Stress?* I don't have any stress-s-s-s—" as he collapses in a heap.

This scenario may seem a bit extreme—and then again, it may not. Yes, we all have stress, usually in more than abundant supply. It's a natural and necessary part of life, but when served in the degrees and quantities many of us face every day, it's no way to live. What can we do about it? What *should* we do about it? The chapters that follow provide some helpful answers.

Chapter 1

Overloaded and Overwhelmed

An interview with Richard A. Swenson, M.D.

Robert J. Tamasy

We talk a lot about what a stressful world we live in today, but a new book argues that the "stressed to the max" individual should not blame society, but himself.

In his book, *Margin: How to Create the Emotional, Physical, Financial, & Time Reserves You Need,* Richard A. Swenson, M.D., contends that much of the stress and overload we carry is self-imposed. We seem compelled to fill every gap in our lives with more expenditures of time, energy, and money.

Ten years ago, Swenson opted to leave the "fraternity of the marginless." He made major lifestyle adjustments—including downscaling his medical practice. This enabled him to escape the bondage of too many commitments. Today, he and his family reside in Menomonie, Wisconsin, and he serves part time on the medical faculty at the University of Wisconsin Medical School. In the following interview, he explains how "margin" relates to stress and tells about steps for restoring margin in life.

/ / /

As a physician, how would you diagnose the state of stress in America today?

Swenson: Stress in society continues to intensify. It's really a threshold phenomenon—until it hit a certain level no one thought much about it. In fact, until the early 1950s, stress was a term only engineers and architects used.

About that time, physiologists discovered that stress has to do with a whole series of hormonal and adrenal changes in the body. Stress is not necessarily bad—it merely describes the body's stress response. When challenges enter our environment, it's important to be able to confront them successfully. As long as we can back out if necessary, stress will not have negative effects. But if we can't, and stresses begin to compound on a daily basis, it can be devastating. This is when "distress" occurs, resulting in a variety of physical, psychological, and emotional consequences.

Are stresses we face today different from those of times past?

One of the things that triggers stress is change. Today we have so much change, at such a great rate, we are unable to compensate. Futurist Alvin Toffler said the disease of the future would be change out of control. We're experiencing this today.

In addition, it is estimated that during our lifetime we have to learn to use twenty thousand pieces of technology, ranging from toasters to VCRs. We have job insecurity, noise, mobility, high indebtedness, and in general, "tight coupling," in which everything is so closely connected that one event starts a chain reaction that can affect the entire country.

How do you define "margin," and how does it relate to stress?

Margin is the difference between your load and your limits. It represents the reserves, space, or leeway that you have—or don't have—in your life.

Like stress, margin is a threshold phenomenon. As long as we have margin in our lives, we don't understand that it's needed. But once it's lost, we feel the anxiety. If we don't maintain some degree of margin in our lives, we won't be happy or healthy.

In Third World countries, the people may be malnourished and have no money—but they have a sense of joy many of us lack. Despite their poverty, they are probably happier than the average American. I'm not saying we should copy their culture, but they clearly show the value of margin in life. They can enjoy a walk or a relaxed conversation without feeling pressed by something more urgent to do.

Has progress cost us contentment and simplicity?

Yes, progress provides many benefits, but it also results in many problems. It invariably leads to increased stress, overload, complexity, speed, change, growth, and debt. I don't suggest that progress be abandoned. But we need antidotes for unanticipated and undesired consequences.

Often the antidote is margin, but it's difficult to obtain and even more difficult to sustain. Most influences in our environment scream for us to maximize. Without contentment and simplicity to counter this, margin has a poor prognosis.

Contentment is both commended and commanded by God. To "accept what we have and to want for little" is a tremendous stress reducer. If we refuse to cultivate contentment as an essential lifestyle component, God has no obligation to assist us with the consequent stress.

As progress moves in the direction of complexity, simplicity can restore life. When we find ourselves overextended in our emotional, financial, and time commitments, simplicity is one of the best ways to reestablish margin. And when we find ourselves flailing about in many directions, simplicity reminds us of the center.

What are indicators of being "marginless"?

Unfortunately, clear indicators often are lacking. The pain is real, sometimes crushing, but the source of the pain is not self-evident.

Marginless people are overloaded, overextended, overworked, and overwhelmed. They are nearly always behind, in debt, or exhausted. Such people show all the characteristic symptoms of stress disorders: depression, anxiety, irritability, withdrawal, worry, fatigue.

In a more generic sense, marginless people are unhappy. They try to do too much too fast with too few resources. As a result, joy disappears and life becomes a weight. Often, regaining joy is as simple (and as difficult) as regaining margin.

You write that "productivity," "efficiency," and "busyness" are overvalued words. Why?

When life is maximized, there is no margin for error. There is also no margin for rest, for healing, for relationships, or for service. No margin even for God.

Productivity, efficiency, and busyness are, at times, appropriate values. But they are speed words, not kingdom words. Very little of lasting emotional or spiritual value happens in the presence of speed. Speed brings stress, not rest.

The Bible never mentions Jesus running. God didn't invent hurry, and neither does He require it of us. In many ways, God is a demanding God, but what He demands is holiness, not exhaustion.

As a physician, which would you advocate most strongly—stress reduction or stress management?

Almost everything written and taught today has to do with stress management. Yet stress reduction is equally important. If you lived in a swamp, I would teach you to swat mosquitoes. But I would also encourage you to move.

What will happen if we actively pursue margin in our lives?

Several things: People enjoy life so much more if they have margin. It permits rest. It nourishes relationships. It enables service to the needs of other people. Physically, it is health enhancing. And spiritually, it allows availability for the purposes of God. When the Lord calls us to do something, He doesn't want to get a busy signal.

Chapter 2

Tomorrow's Anxieties Today

How to deal with anxiety and pressure

Henry J. Miltenberger Jr.

It's midafternoon. You still have a contract to review, two letters that have to get out, and five calls to return before leaving town tomorrow. An irate client calls with a problem that needs to be handled now. Some bills are due, but your checking account is almost overdrawn. You forgot to take care of trip cash, you haven't looked at your priority mail, and an internal office conflict arises that can't wait until you come back.

To top it off, your child's science project is due in three days, so you need to get home on time to help. You remember that before leaving you wanted to make reservations for your anniversary, which is next week. You begin to feel desperate.

This is how we live. The velocity of life and pressures from hundreds of competing demands drive us. The future appears so uncertain, who can help but worry? And there is no end in sight. It's a hard world for a born worrier like me, someone whose sixth grade teacher warned my parents that I worried too much.

At issue here is not stress, but distress. When stress "gets to us" and causes loss of peace, joy, and perspective, it becomes sin. This is when we violate Matthew 6:34: "Therefore do not be anxious for tomorrow, for tomorrow will care for itself. Each day has enough trouble of its own" (NASB).

High Anxiety

I run an insurance third-party administration firm with a heavy emphasis on medical coverage. Relentless medical cost trends have led to a crisis. Proposed state and federal solutions likely will create more problems for our clients—and certainly for us. I *should* be worried! How can we "rejoice in our tribulations," as the apostle Paul states in Romans 5:3?

It was interesting to learn that this Greek word for *tribulation* is used to describe being pressed by a crowd of people; it could easily be translated as pressure or stress. Even in the first century, the apostle was writing for life in the twentieth century. But how can we turn this pressure—or distress—into joy?

First, we need to understand where anxious feelings come from.

Expectations

We all have a tendency to plan as though life were predictable. I think I can work until 6:00 P.M., drive home, go for a quick fifteen-minute run, shower, grab dinner, and make the show at 7:00. But when something happens to hold me in the office until 6:10, I get anxious. I don't expect the unexpected!

Another example of improper expectations arises from a lack of contentment. I want a life like I see in TV commercials. I often forget that God owns and controls "my" finances and possessions. When I worry about acquiring and achieving, I need to review Philippians 4:6–7, which tells me not to be anxious about anything. Instead, as I submit my concerns to God in prayer, He will grant me peace "which transcends all understanding."

Self-Reliance

Pride has many faces. One of those faces might be the belief that we can handle any situation. We often put pressure on ourselves to achieve given results, when the outcome is actually in the hands of God. Since we wrongly believe the results depend on us, we begin to worry—and experience negative stress.

Unbiblical View of the World

We forget that we have a sovereign God who is in absolute control of all circumstances. No one can "hurt" me outside of the Lord's will. Therefore, the only two people I need to worry about are God and me. If I truly believe God loves me and desires the best for me, then the only person I need to worry about is me! But if I doubt His sovereignty, I will worry about what others will do to me. And fear of man is a snare.

Debt Pressure

In our rush to top last year's standard of living, trying to keep up with or surpass our neighbors and our parents, we spend next year's income by borrowing. This is presumption. Trying to meet accumulated debt obligations only adds to our worries.

Getting Rid of Stress

Focus on God

What's the solution? First, when we are anxious—not just concerned, but overconcerned—with tomorrow, it's sin. We need to admit it and confess it to God. It's impossible to be *still* and know that He is God (Ps. 46:10) when we are filled with anxiety. Distress often arises out of presumption, hopes fixed on the temporal, poor stewardship, lack of contentment, and lack of faith.

This lack of faith is the greatest cause of distress. A few years ago, my company was on the verge of losing a major client. We had done all we could, but I was worried. I simply didn't trust God to act in our best interest.

I would often quote Romans 8:28, which tells us that all things work together for good, but I wasn't sure that God's definition for "good" was the same as mine. I preferred my own, which included a new car, a prospering business, and a child who wins the science fair.

When we acknowledge our weak faith, we need to comply with 1 Peter 5:7: "Casting all your anxiety upon Him, because He cares for you" (NASB).

Trust God to Do His Part

Writing my concerns on paper helped me to turn them over to God and seek His help. The next step is to separate my part from His part, and trust Him to do His. In the Old Testament, we read that God always told Israel to obey Him; He would do the worrying about their enemies. Every time they disobeyed, they got into trouble.

In Luke 8:22–25, we see the anxiety of Jesus' disciples. Frankly, if I were caught on a small boat in a big storm, I would worry too. But after calming the storm, Jesus rebuked them, asking, "Where is your faith?" We face similar storms—a tree falling on your house, proposed legislation that would be disastrous to our businesses, or looming deadlines at the office.

One thing I have learned is that they are brought into my life by God, to be used in His refining process for me. Since He works all things together for our good, there is no reason to worry. God holds the future—that's His part.

Do Your Part

Then what is our part? To set godly priorities, to work hard, to respond to circumstances with an attitude of joy and peace, and to leave the controls to God. For instance, as I have tried to reduce stress in my life, I have sought God's will on how much time I should spend at work. Now, when the time comes to go home, I go. This is possible, however, only if I really trust God.

If I believe the future depends on me, then I better buy a cot for my office.

Stress in our lives could be substantially reduced if we realized our reason for being here is not to live in a great neighborhood or to save up so we can retire comfortably and see Europe. Jesus came to give His life to others, and in Luke 9:23 He says, "If anyone wishes to come after Me, let him deny himself, and take up his cross daily, and follow Me" (NASB).

Whose Plans Are They?

He calls us to die to our ambitions and expectations, but this isn't bad because they are major causes of stress in our lives. Instead, we are to be available to serve as He directs—even when it puts carefully laid plans and desires in jeopardy.

Do we trust God? He wasn't kidding when He said in Hebrews 4:3, "We who have believed enter that rest" (NASB).

Rest, the absence of anxiety, can only come from trusting God enough to obey, even when circumstances don't seem to make obedience a reasonable course of action. We need to pursue God's will as best as we can discern it, then live one day at a time. Tomorrow belongs to Him. And as we all know, each day *does* have enough trouble of its own!

Chapter 3

Stress that Motivates

Responding positively to negative circumstances

Dru Scott Decker

The mugs of steaming coffee at our breakfast meeting had barely been filled when my colleague across the table blurted out, "I don't want to hear that word one more time. Why do we have all this talk about stress? Why don't they just get the job done?"

Today, the word *stress* is tossed around with such frequency, it is hard to go to a meeting without someone mentioning it. In contrast, twenty years ago, I am sure I would not have found an issue of a business magazine that spotlighted stress. What is behind this shift—and what can we do about it?

Stress is increasing because the rate and frequency of change is increasing—dramatically. Hans Selye, M.D., defined stress as "the nonspecific response of the body to any demand made upon it."[1] This classic definition in *Stress Without Distress* spotlights change and the demands it makes on people to adapt. Since change is so closely linked with stress, let's look at changes confronting us.

Bankruptcies. Mergers. Debt. Each week headlines scream about massive layoffs and plant closures. Companies that were once household names have become as extinct as dinosaurs. Change is all around us. That means invitations to stress are all around us.

Tools for managing stress have never been more urgently needed than right now. Surviving in the stressful environment of the 1990s calls for knowing how to respond to stress effectively and how to transform stress into motivation. This is true for individuals and for organizations.

Competition is fierce. The global economy is zigzagging on an uncharted course. The job market looks like a high-stakes game of musical chairs. People wonder where they will be when the music stops.

Whether people own the company or work in the mail room, their future depends on their ability to create value, deliver quality, and build a reputation for excellence. As Peter F. Drucker emphasizes in *Managing for the Future*, "Businesses will undergo more, and more radical, restructuring in the 1990s than at any time since the modern corporate organization first evolved in the 1920s."[2] These demands and changes add up to each of us having a greater need to keep our own motivation high and to understand stress.

For a popular definition, think of stress as those forces that hinder people from moving in their chosen directions. Many people regard stress as draining and deflecting, and motivation as leading and lifting.

For a more specific definition, consider Dr. Selye's approach more closely: "the nonspecific response of the body to any demand made upon it." Demands can be pleasant or unpleasant. And demands for change add up.

Facing It and Taking It On

What complicates the situation is that few people have been taught to believe that they can always face a demand, take purposeful action, and make some improvement. If they believe, "There is nothing I can do," they become mired in the quicksand of nonspecific responses. Few people have learned the damaging implications of this belief.

"Most stress is caused by our belief systems," says Paul Ware, M.D., a teacher of behavioral medicine, psychoanalyst and neurologist at Louisiana State University, and the head of a psychiatric clinic in Shreveport, Louisiana.

"Our choices and the ways we perceive and react to life experiences cause the bulk of our stress," according to Dr. Ware. "So much of stress has to do with people's belief systems. And we *can* change our belief systems. The person who learned early in life to think, 'I can solve problems,' or 'I can figure things out' has less stress than most people. The person who didn't learn this belief as a child can learn it as an adult."

Our belief systems do influence our stress—and our motivation.

Some people believe that *motivation* means enthusiasm or happiness. However, we are talking about something specific and dynamic, a driving force that draws us toward achievement and fulfillment.

> *If a change or demand confronts us, and we deny it or do nothing, we have stress that damages.*
>
> *However, when we respond to a change or demand by taking purposeful action, we have stress that motivates.*
>
> Dru Scott Decker
> *Stress That Motivates*

Pictures of Where You Need to Go

The motivated person does not fall into the trap of merely seeing what surrounds him. The motivated person fills his mind with targets, objectives, and pictures of excellence. The motivated person pictures his or her destinations daily.

The Bible encourages us not to be limited to what we see with our eyes. It tells us the importance of "being sure" of the goals and destinations that God gives us. Remember Hebrews 11:1. "Now faith is being sure of what we hope for and certain of what we do not see." We are not limited by our external circumstances.

I will never forget the power of being certain of what we do not see with our physical eyes. This principle flashes in my mind when I think about my sister-in-law, Carol, when she faced a stressful situation. She had faith. She developed a new picture. She took action. She also shared the picture. And she helped everyone take steps toward it.

Pops and the Power of a Picture

"This idea isn't just for work. It's effective at home, too," Carol concluded to all of us around the table at our breakfast meeting.

"I saw it turn around a sad situation in my home." A publishing executive in her early forties, Carol swung around to face the rest of us at the end of the table as she continued. "It was a devastating moment for our family. The doctor had just whispered the latest on Pops' diagnosis. As we stood there in the hall listening, I shook my head. It couldn't be.

"Even at seventy-nine, my husband's father was still so interested in life. He read the news. Every day. He called his five children. Every Sunday. He balanced his checking account. Every month and on the day the statement arrived. The doctor had to be wrong. Pops couldn't just have 'weeks to live.'"

Carol hesitated, looked away briefly, then smiled and straightened the yellow-lined pad in front of her. "Pops was always doing something. Going somewhere. Or helping someone get somewhere.

"He had a ritual. As soon as each grandchild started middle school, Pops started talking about 'writing a résumé.' He made sure all of the kids started seeing themselves graduating from college. Using a résumé. Finding a good job. Pops would always find opportunities to be a cheerleader to each grandchild. 'You can do it. It's good for the résumé.'"

Carol related that this image was just one of the memories tumbling through her mind as she kept hoping the doctor didn't have the right diagnosis. "'Living on oxygen and borrowed time.' That's what the doctor said." She couldn't bear the thought that Pops would only be with them a few more weeks.

Carol swallowed, looked down, then across the table. She caught my eye for a moment as she continued. "One evening it hit me. I had taken Pops' dinner tray upstairs to our guest room as usual. He joked as usual. He teased me as usual. Told me I was a blonde bombshell."

Something to Work Toward

"As I joked with him, my eye caught his bedside table and the stack of family photo albums. Pops had spent hours organizing them—first by kids' families, then by themes, then by years. It was a big project. That's when it struck me.

"Pops' was always motivated by having a big project, something big to work toward.

"So as I sat there on the side of his bed, I handed him a challenge. 'Pops, you can't take it with you. Why don't you throw a family reunion? We'll all celebrate your eightieth birthday a year from now. Invite all the kids. The grandkids, too. And Pops, what about you paying for the party and the travel for everyone?'

"Even though he was weak and on oxygen most of the time, Pops kept at it. Tracking down the best air fares. Planning the meals. Picking out the awards for the contests. Checking how grandchildren wanted to share rooms. Deciding how teams would play in the basketball contest. Seeing to each detail of the event. Pops spent the entire year organizing the family reunion.

"The doctor was amazed. We were delighted. Pops was smiling. All twenty-seven of us were at his birthday reunion. We wrote poems for his scrapbook. We rehearsed skits for his dinner. We toasted him. We teased him.

"Even though Pops was on oxygen all the time and had to be carried down the stairs in his wheelchair, it was a great event.

"I know what did it—what gave us the pleasure of an extra year of his life. It wasn't just his courage. It wasn't just his character. It was seeing his dream."

When Carol finished sharing her story, I told myself again: *We all have changes. We all have stresses. And we all have choices. Don't blame and wait. Face the situation. Picture where you want to go. Take a step forward. Then take another step.*

Adapted with permission from *Stress That Motivates*
by Dru Scott Decker
copyright 1992, Crisp Publications, Inc.,
(Menlo Park, Calif. All rights reserved.)

---

1. Hans Selye, M.D., *Stress Without Distress* (Philadelphia: J. B. Lippincott Co., 1974).

2. Peter F. Drucker, *Managing for the Future* (New York: Truman Talley Books / Dalton, 1992).

Chapter 4

Rx from the Great Physician

Sometimes a rest is simply for the best

Robert J. Tamasy

Did you ever feel totally, undeniably tapped out, having given all that you had to give—unable to give any more? I suspect we all have experienced a time or two like that. Deadlines at work, demands at home, even self-inflicted pressures often leave us feeling depleted physically, mentally, emotionally—and spiritually.

A contemporary term for this condition is being "stressed out." Circumstances, responsibilities, and expectations unavoidably line up and require us to fly as long and high and far as we can, until the time comes when a landing is necessary. Some people have another term for this—"crash." The trick is to avoid the more serious counterpart, "crash and burn."

I can remember once when my life seemed so overloaded that I began to feel a real empathy for the camel that panicked when confronted by the back-breaking straw. "If just one more thing happens, I'll. . . ."

What can we do at times like these? There are many alternatives. We can crawl into a corner, fold our bodies into a fetal position, and suck our thumbs. (Not terribly creative, but some people have tried it.)

We can stay in bed, pull the covers over our heads, and hope that things will be better in the morning—or next week. (Chances are, they won't be.)

We can run screaming through our neighborhood. (Do this, however, and you might find yourself assigned to another "neighborhood" until your behavior is more appropriate for public display.)

Breaking Routine

Perhaps a far better solution, if possible, is a vacation—a complete break from the routine, even if only for a few days. Time to clear your head, gain a fresh perspective, regroup body and spirit, and then return to the fray—hopefully with renewed energy and enthusiasm. In fact, vacations have biblical precedents.

Consider the example of the prophet Elijah in 1 Kings 18–19. The situation was this: One lone prophet of the true God Jehovah against 450 prophets of the false god, Baal. (Outnumbered by a prophet-making organization!)

You might recall the unusual duel Elijah proposed. Both sides would carve up a bull, lay it on the altar of wood, then call on their respective deities to consume the animal sacrifice. Elijah, a true gentleman, even said, "You guys go first."

As expected, the false god did nothing, even though the prophets went to the trouble of mutilating themselves. No barbecue for these pagans!

Finally, Elijah declared, "Okay. My turn." After building an altar of twelve stones with wood on top and digging a trench around it, he drenched the offering and the wood with water three times, flooding the trench. Then Elijah prayed, asking God to respond.

First Fire

The Lord's answer was immediate, sending fire to consume the sacrifice, the wood, the stones, the soil, even the water in the trench. Instantly, all the witnesses knew the answer to the question, "Which is the true God?"

On the heels of this miraculous display, Elijah participated in another bold act. He commanded that all the prophets of Baal be executed. What a death sentence to pronounce!

Then Rain

Even at this, the prophet's work still was not done. He forecast a 100 percent chance of rain, apparent foolishness in a region that had suffered through several years of drought. No clouds were in sight, and the skeptics were probably laughing hysterically. "He may be a prophet, but he sure isn't a weatherman." Yet God responded with another miracle—a heavy rainstorm that sent everyone scrambling for cover.

Then, Jezebel!

After events like these, how could anyone *ever* doubt God again? But when he heard that wicked Queen Jezebel was plotting to avenge the deaths of her pet prophets, Elijah muttered something like, "I can't take it anymore. I'm outta here!" He fled and prayed that God would let him die.

"Overreacting a bit, aren't you, Elijah?" we want to ask. "After all you have seen God do, don't you think He can handle one mean ole queen?"

Was this simply an example of weak faith? Well, Elijah had enough faith for the fire and for the rain. I think he was simply stressed out. Can you imagine the emotions he must have felt, waiting for the miracles to occur? Excitement. Anticipation. A rush of joy at seeing the Lord demonstrate His faithfulness in such dramatic ways. Adrenaline, which we know today as a primary stress hormone, must have been surging through his body all day.

After reaching such an emotional peak, Elijah must have been ready to wind down and reflect on what God had done. But then came yet another crisis. The poor prophet, maxed out and too exhausted to fight, elected to flee.

Finding God in the Calm

How did God respond? Rather than chastising Elijah, denouncing him as a backslider or worse, the Lord sent a ministering angel. He provided food and water, and allowed him to get plenty of sleep, never once rebuking him. God sent an earthquake, a whirlwind, and a fire, then finally addressed Elijah—in a gentle whisper. After all the chaos, Elijah found God still living in the calm.

Their dialogue was simple. God asked, "What are you doing here, Elijah?" The prophet recounted how he had stood up for the Lord and then concluded, "I am the only one left, and now they are trying to kill me too."

At this point, without anger, God seems to smile at Elijah and reply, "No, it only seems that way. Actually I have seven thousand more servants just as faithful as you. Come on, now. I have given you time to rest up and become restored. It's time to get back in the battle." And Elijah goes.

He Knows Our Limits

In my view, this is one of the most encouraging passages in the Bible. It says that God understands when we reach our limits. He's not shocked. As the psalmist writes, "he remembers that we are dust" (Ps. 103:14). When circumstances gang up on us and we are forced to call a hasty timeout, the Lord says it's okay. After all, when Jesus walked the earth, He had times when He needed to withdraw from the crush of the crowd and the drain of continual demands.

Sometimes in business we may feel like Elijah, as if we are the only ones left, that everyone else is worshiping false gods. But as we step back to regroup, the Lord reminds us we are not alone. "I have many more who also love and serve Me. Numerically, you may be in the minority, but remember—any minority plus God equals a majority."

Not All Things All the Time

An extremely encouraging verse is Philippians 4:13, which says, "I can do all things through Him who strengthens me" (NASB). Perhaps even more interesting is what it does *not* say. It doesn't say that we will be able to do all things *all the time*. Nor does it say that we will never get tired, weak, or just plain worn out. In fact, the unique demands of the committed Christian life may inevitably lead us to an occasion when our tank has run dry. A swift retreat may be our only recourse, the prescription from the Great Physician.

But as we see in the life of Elijah, this does not mean we are washed up and cast aside, of no further use to God. Just as the prophet recharged and then returned to fulfilling his godly calling, we too can pause, refresh, and return to the place where the Lord has called us to serve and represent Him.

Recognizing our fragile physical and emotional states, God included the observance of the Sabbath as one of His Ten Commandments. Jesus also noted, however, "The Sabbath was made for man, not man for the Sabbath" (Mark 2:27). If the stresses in your life start to go off the chart, you might need to extend the Sabbath beyond a day or two. Allow the Lord to restore you, and then get back in the race. It matters not who is in the lead; what does matter is whether you finish.

*Therefore, since we are receiving a
kingdom that cannot be shaken,
let us be thankful.*

—Hebrews 12: 28

Coping with Change

*T*he more things change, the more they stay the same." So goes
the old saying, but today it seems the only thing that remains
the same is that everything is changing. And the rate of change
is ever-increasing. Thanks in part to modern technology, change
comes at us faster than we can deal with it.

If you buy a home computer, chances are good that within
months—even weeks—it will be obsolete, outdated by another
more advanced machine. Watches, TVs, and cars offer standard
features we could not have imagined ten years ago. Fax machines,
voice mail, and car phones are rapidly moving from luxury status
to necessities.

But technology is not the only change catalyst. The business
world has turned upside down, with corporate giants battling to
maintain a competitive edge, while upstart newcomers keep
changing the rules of the game. If you don't like your company,
be patient. It will probably be bought out, merge with another
firm, or undergo a drastic makeover.

Politically and economically, the scenery changes so frequently we can scarcely get a picture of it. In every area of society, from the family to the media, from sports to religion, things just aren't the same. And the way they are today probably won't be how they are tomorrow.

So how do we cope with all this change? Obviously, we can't stop the world and get off, so we're stuck with facing the realities of change, seeking to understand its causes, and adapting as best—and quickly—as we can. In the 1960s, folk musician Bob Dylan wrote the song, "The Times They Are A-Changin'." This is even more true today. Either we learn how to cope with change, or we get buried under it.

Chapter 5

Surviving the Merger

Alexander S. Williams

Merger. This simple word stirs emotions ranging from delight to dread. Terms like *reorganization* and *downsizing* have a similar effect. At best, they mean things are going to change, perhaps drastically. At worst, they mean people are going to lose their jobs, maybe many of them—maybe even you.

My first experience with a merger occurred in February 1988. The bank where I worked, First Fidelity Bank in Newark, New Jersey, merged with Fidelity Bank of Philadelphia. Since then, change has become a way of life. Of the approximately twenty-five senior bank officers back in 1988, only three of us are left. We have gone through three total changes of management.

Everyone involved in a merger experiences a mixture of feelings. There are new rules and procedures, new people to report to. Insecurity and financial concerns are common.

Disillusionment also occurs. Years ago, middle and senior managers in the corporate environment relied on the perceived security of an unwritten "contract": they essentially sold their skills and the employer bought them. It was the nature of the deal. Employees assumed that job security was part of the contract. In the 1980s and 1990s, however, we discovered this so-called contract never really existed, that we had just kidded ourselves that it was there.

In my case, I have been able to weather the changes. My department, First Fidelity Securities Group, a medium-sized broker/dealer affiliated with the bank, has continued to do well. But today, even success does not guarantee job security.

When the merger first occurred, a man at Fidelity had a position similar to my own. Obviously, we couldn't both hold the same job, and I wound up reporting to him.

You learn not to be so attached to your job. For many executives, this means developing a "pink-slip contingency plan," making sure that your finances can withstand a period of unemployment if necessary.

While this is practical, it's still not easy because our vocations play an important part in defining who we are. A couple of factors have helped me to cope with the uncertainties of my job, along with the ongoing changes.

Ready to Respond, Willing to Risk

One factor relates to my work background before going into banking in 1970. I had been a municipal bond trader in New York City for about fifteen years. Talk about living with change and uncertainty! I compare bond traders to fighter pilots: You have few encounters, but those you have are very intense as you move in for the kill. Moments of concerted activity are combined with long periods of extreme boredom during dull markets.

The bond trader, like the fighter pilot, must be aggressive and quick to react without knowing for certain what the results will be, running the risk that he could get shot down in flames.

It has been more than twenty years since I left that business, but things are not much different today. In fact, the stakes have gotten much bigger and the pace a lot faster, so the burnout rate is higher. Like pilots, there are not many traders over the age of thirty-five.

A Life-Changing Faith

I was close to burnout in 1970. Wondering what to do with the rest of my life, it occurred to me that at one end of Wall Street was the East River and on the other end was Trinity Church. For some reason, I concluded that the church was a better alternative, even though I didn't believe in God.

This initiated the second factor—a spiritual pilgrimage that continued for seventeen years until I committed my life to Jesus Christ through a Bible study at Drew University. Several months later, I was introduced to the Christian Business Men's Committee, and through CBMC I began to understand the relationship between my faith and work.

The fact that this occurred about the same time as the merger was not coincidence. God had been trying to get my attention for years; I finally realized I needed something more stable to rely on than my job.

My faith has provided purpose and meaning that no corporate position could ever offer, along with strength and confidence for dealing with the inevitable ups and downs of the changing business climate.

This doesn't mean things don't get to me. I still have a long way to go as a Christian, but I always come back to the fact that God loves me and whatever happens is part of his unique plan for me and my family.

The insurance company's commercial urges us to "get a piece of the rock," but the Bible teaches that "there is no Rock like our God" (1 Sam. 2:2). That is the kind of assurance that people in business need today.

Chapter 6

Overcoming an Age-old Problem

Preparing for employee reactions to change

Millard N. MacAdam

There are times when a change of direction in a company is desirable, perhaps even inevitable. Hopefully these changes are planned, timely, and in everyone's best interest. To ensure success, corporate directional changes must be guided by people of character, competence, and commitment.

Usually change is unsettling and sometimes traumatic. For this reason, it's essential to be sensitive to how the change will affect individuals in your organization. As Proverbs 27:23 tells us, "Be sure you know the condition of your flocks, give careful attention to your herds." The Bible exhorts that we are to "be shepherds of God's flock that is under your care" (1 Pet. 5:2), and I believe this applies to business settings as much as anywhere else.

Therefore, we need to recognize that any kind of change can have a detrimental impact on people who work with us and for us, unless the change process is introduced and implemented with care. Formulating a new vision, a set of driving values, a mission, or goals, constitutes significant change. So do new performance standards, policies, or procedures, a new computer system, or relocation of your business.

When initiating any type of change that affects people, let me suggest some proven principles for success. They will keep your company's "ship" from veering dangerously off course or sinking because of poor planning and execution of specific changes.

Implementing Change Successfully

▲ Involve in planning for the change those who will be helping to carry out the change.

▲ Clearly define people's roles in the change, goals of the change, and how achievement of the goals will be evaluated.

▲ Express in writing the goals and objectives for the change and circulate them to everyone who will assist in implementing the change.

▲ Address people's needs! Disrupt only what is necessary for accomplishing your goals for the change. Whenever possible, avoid disrupting positive elements such as friendships, familiar work settings, personally preferred work procedures, and group norms.

▲ Design flexibility into the change process. Don't redirect your course too quickly or people may panic, causing your "ship" to hit rocks and sink. Allow them to complete current efforts and provide time for them to assimilate new skills, procedures, support mechanisms, and work behaviors needed to successfully institute the change.

▲ Look for areas of agreement between yourself, as a leading orchestrator of the change, and those who oppose it.

▲ Focus on the positive aspects and benefits of the change whenever possible.

▲ Establish parameters and define the limits of the change.

▲ Design adequate training and allow mental and emotional adjustment time for the people involved.

Overcoming Resistance to Change

Most people feel anxious about change. It's normal. Whenever you initiate change, resistance will surface—count on it. The goal is to channel and manage this opposition, helping people move to new levels of excellence and service.

In coaching leaders in companies of all sizes through the change process, I have observed some common causes of resistance:

▲ Goals and benefits of change not accepted

▲ Benefits of change not communicated

▲ Fear of the unknown

▲ Fear of failure

▲ Dislike for person recommending the change

▲ Wrong timing

▲ Belief that it will only make the boss look good

▲ Fear of having to work harder

▲ Fear of loss of rights or status

I also have seen some people's resistance turn into defensiveness, then to toxic attack. It's tough for managers to stabilize change when people sabotage operations, blow up emotionally at others, and steal time or materials out of anger. Or when they exhibit aggressive, overt resistance, with blaming and finger pointing. Or when they moan and groan, withhold support, fence-sit, or offer outward agreement to the changes but do not demonstrate a commitment to making the change happen.

You can avoid or overcome such toxic behaviors by strategically leading people through the change process without creating organizational chaos. To do so requires focusing on people's "will do" stage of *concern* about the new change and their "can do" level of *competency* or existing knowledge and skills they have for supporting and successfully implementing the new change.

Determining the "will do" motivated stage of concern is a critical first step before initiating change, even when people possess the needed "can do" competencies. To effectively lead others through successful change efforts, leaders must:

▲ Recognize behaviors indicative of the *seven stages of concern* (see the list below) that people have regarding specific changes.

▲ Interview each individual affected by the coming change, establish rapport, and determine their stage of concern.

▲ Use proven leadership and communication strategies to influence, inspire, encourage, and coach each person, helping to reduce their concerns and ensure that they have the "can do" skills for putting the change into effect.

Remember, emotion usually controls logic and action. Concerns are emotional. If you address them first with each person within your sphere of leadership, you will find making changes of any type in your company to be easier, faster, and more successful. As a leader and manager, your life also will be more satisfying because you won't have to endure the hassle and stress of "revolting" people.

Seven Stages of Concern

Each person involved in a corporate change can be found in one of the *Seven Stages of Concern*. These stages have been identified by Gene E. Hall and his research colleagues at the University of Texas-Austin. I have found that the seven stages included in Hall's change model apply to people involved in corporate change.

Recognizing and understanding these seven change stages helps in addressing individual needs. It is important to determine which stage people are in, so you can properly respond to their concerns.

Use a simple, informal interview process to obtain the information you need. As you talk to the people, listen to what they are saying and try to understand their underlying emotions. Pay special attention to their non-verbal behavior. In this way, you can determine how best to help them overcome their concerns before changes are made.

Awareness is the first stage. The person exhibits little concern about the change or involvement with it.

Informational is the second stage. The person has a general awareness of the change and desires to know more details about it. The person seems unworried personally and is primarily interested in substantive aspects of the change.

Personal is the third stage. Here the individual is uncertain about the demands of the change, personal adequacy to meet those demands, and his or her role in the change. This includes analysis of relationship to the reward structure of the organization, decision making, and consideration of potential conflicts with existing structures or colleagues.

Managerial is the fourth stage. A person's attention is focused on the processes and tasks of implementing the change and the best use of information and resources. Concerns relate to efficiency, organizing, managing, scheduling, and time demands.

Consequence is the fifth stage. The person's attention here focuses on the impact and relevance of the change on his or her immediate sphere of influence, including performance, competencies, and adjustments needed to increase employee and organizational effectiveness.

Collaboration is the sixth stage. The focus here is the person's coordination and cooperation with others regarding implementation of the change.

Refocusing is the seventh stage. This concern relates to exploring more universal benefits from the change, including the possibility of additional changes.

By relating sensitively to your people with the insights gained through informal interviews to uncover their concerns, you can reduce anxiety and chaos by coaching and guiding them through company changes.

If a person's concerns about the change are high, that is not the time to send them to skills development activities to enhance their competencies. Address their concerns first, relieving fears and overcoming resistance, then deal with developing the skills needed for them to successfully participate in the change process.

Chapter 7

Getting an Edge on the Future

An interview with Joel Barker

Robert J. Tamasy

In 1970, Alvin Toffler published *Future Shock*, which described the response of a society struggling to cope with the continually escalating pace of change in the latter stages of the twentieth century. Joel Arthur Barker, in his book *Future Edge*, exposes a primary cause for this severe reaction: paradigms.

Futurist Barker says the word *paradigm* comes from the Greek *paradeigma*, which means "model, pattern, example." He defines a paradigm as "a set of rules and regulations (written or unwritten) that does two things: (1) establishes or defines boundaries; and (2) tells you how to behave inside the boundaries in order to be successful."[1]

According to Barker, we each have a unique collection of paradigms that govern how we understand, interpret, and respond to information and events. These paradigms formulate our "comfort zone," whether at work, in our homes, in worship, or any other environment. The problem occurs when a paradigm "shifts." Suddenly we find ourselves in a new game, faced with a new set of rules.

"When a paradigm shifts, we all go back to zero," he writes. For those of us who dislike change, our reaction can range from annoyance to consternation to utter confusion.

The Quartz Quandary

In *Future Edge,* Barker cites the classic example of the quartz watch. The electronic quartz movement was developed in the research institute in Neuchatel, Switzerland. However, since it didn't look like a watch, act like a watch, or sound like a watch—as the Swiss knew it—they essentially concluded that it must not *be* a watch. This was in 1968. The power of 20/20 hindsight allows us to sum up that conclusion in one word: *wrong!*

Later that year, the quartz prototype was displayed at an international watch-making congress. The Japanese, seeing how the quartz watch concept fit in with new electronic technology, took one look and it was love at first sight. In 1968, the Japanese had less than 1 percent of the world's watch market. Today, they own about one-third of the market, while by 1980 the Swiss share had dropped from 65 percent to 10 percent.

How could such a thing happen? It was simply a case of different paradigms. To the Swiss, the definition of a watch had very narrowly defined boundaries, which caused them to miss the significance of the quartz invention. The Japanese, not affected with similar limitations, saw the first quartz watch and immediately thought, *Why not?*

What does this have to do with us? Just this: We live in a time of unprecedented change, and the rate at which this change is taking place is speeding up, not slowing down. Success in the future will relate directly to our ability to cope with all of this change, and to a large extent this means being able to break out of old, outmoded paradigms.

Information Explosion

Roger Selbert, another futurist, predicts that although the total amount of information we have today is vast, that information will amount to only *3 percent* of all the information that will be available to us in the year 2010!2 Imagine the changes this will bring about.

Companies and organizations that stay on the cutting edge of change will be the survivors and successes of the twenty-first century. Those which cling to old paradigms because "we have always done it this way" will become the twentieth century answers to the dinosaur.

Need to Integrate Changes

Obviously, computers and related technology will pave the way for much of this change. On an individual level, our ability to adjust and integrate these changes—some of them very dramatic—will greatly affect our impact in society.

Some of us will be paradigm "shifters," those who become directly involved in the process of changing from one paradigm to another. Others will be paradigm "pioneers," who recognize that a new path has been blazed and are among the first to follow it. Then there will be what Barker calls the paradigm "settlers," the cautious, conservative types who wait for the "all-clear" signal before letting go of one paradigm and grabbing hold of another. Unfortunately, before they finish getting settled, they may discover with some dismay that the "new" paradigm is already out of date!

While *Future Edge* does not address spiritual concerns, the ramifications for Christians are considerable. For instance, many church traditions and forms are already outliving their usefulness. If the church is to remain relevant to a society in continual flux, it must be flexible—without compromising the basic tenets, the "unchanging paradigms," of the faith. Books like George Barna's *The Frog in the Kettle,* Jim Petersen's *Church Without*

Walls, and Leith Anderson's *Dying for Change* and *A Church for the 21st Century* explore many of these issues.

Formidable Task

In the business world, the task of communicating the Christian faith in a meaningful and practical way is formidable. The Christian Business Men's Committee, for example, has implemented numerous innovations over its sixty-plus years, and there are many more to come.

With our country rapidly losing touch with its Judeo-Christian heritage (the old paradigm) and becoming more secular (the new paradigm), the "basics" must become even more basic if the truth of Jesus Christ (the unchanging paradigm) is to be clearly presented.

Perhaps the greatest—and most important—challenge of all will be to affirm and demonstrate that the Christ of the first century is just as much the Christ of the twenty-first!

Three Keys to Success in the Twenty-first Century

One of the most successful business videos in recent years has been *Discovering the Future: The Business of Paradigms,* in which futurist Joel Arthur Barker explains how old ways of thinking can blind us to the value and benefits of change. He is completing a four-part series of videos that explores the sequence of paradigm change in greater depth.

Barker is president of Infinity Limited, Inc. of St. Paul, Minnesota, an internationally known consulting firm that pioneered the concept of strategic exploration, working with top management teams of Fortune 500 companies.

In the interview that follows, Barker explains why he believes a clear understanding of the change process is so vital to success in the future.

///

In your book, Future Edge, *you write that the three keys to the future for any organization that wants to participate fully in the twenty-first century are anticipation, innovation, and excellence. How do these relate to your discussion of paradigms?*

Barker: It's important to note that excellence is at the base of the list because it is the base of the twenty-first century, whether it is in winning awards or simply living up to your own standards. This will be the most important paradigm shift in the next century.

Today, companies are looking at excellence as a competitive edge, but in the twenty-first century it will become the necessary price of entry. What this means, essentially, is trying to do better tomorrow than you did today. The Japanese call this *kaizen.* On a personal level, this means honoring yourself because it acknowledges your capacity to grow and improve. This is, in reality, very much Christian.

In what ways?

Jesus asked us to hold to the three basic rules that He gave—to love God above all else, to love our neighbor as ourselves, and to do unto others as we would have them to do unto us. I see these in progression, building upon one another and giving our lives of faith great substance and meaning.

In fractal mathematics, you start with a very simple pattern, but as the pattern keeps repeating itself, it develops into wonderfully beautiful and complex patterns. As Christians strive to follow Jesus' three basic commands—His pattern for excellence—we too take part in something of increasing beauty and complexity.

Why do you place innovation on top of the base of excellence?

Innovation is all about progress. If you're not innovative, you start to practice obsolete excellence. Innovation says we are creative, clever, smart, and always looking for better ways of doing things. God made this world so complex, we should never get bored of looking for different ways of solving problems. For instance, there may be 60 million solutions for our environmental problems. I see innovation as our way of interacting with God's gifts, seeing more and more of the beauty God created.

And above these you place anticipation?

Yes, this is all about why we innovate. This answers questions such as "Why are we here?" and "What is my role in the world?" Anticipating the future is our way of finding the right pathway. If we can know in advance and choose the best way, then we can be most efficient in our use of resources.

How important do you think understanding paradigms will be to America's future?

We used to be the greatest paradigm shifters and paradigm pioneers, but lately we shifted the paradigms but left the pioneering to other nations. Paradigm pioneers follow the rough pathway the paradigm shifters have uncovered.

Think of some of the paradigm changes we left for others to pioneer—the video-tape recorder, microwave ovens, color TV, and fax machines. We essentially gave all of these ideas away.

Why would we do this?

In the last fifteen years, the people at the top of organizations have been looking for safety, managing with an accountant's mentality. They are settlers, not pioneers, moving ahead only when they are sure it's safe. Unfortunately, when a paradigm shifts, "safe" is too late.

Paradigm pioneers never wait for numbers to justify their actions. We have crippled ourselves by giving too much attention to safety, by trying to protect what we already have. In the process, we jeopardize the future.

1. Joel Arthur Barker, *Future Edge* (New York: Wm. Morrow & Co., Inc, 1992).
2. In George Barna's *The Frog in the Kettle* (Ventura, Calif.: Regal Books, 1990).

Chapter 8

L.A. Justice

Coping with career loss

Robert J. Tamasy

On May 2, 1992, Robert Vernon was in Fort Lauderdale, Florida, attending a Christian businessmen's conference; 2,700 miles away, Los Angeles burned.

In a sense, it seemed as if Vernon's own heart was on fire. For more than thirty-seven years, he had invested much of his life in the Los Angeles Police Department, a career he loved. Only a week earlier, he had reluctantly retired as assistant police chief. It was particularly painful knowing that the widespread violence and destruction inflicted upon the city's midsection had grown out of the acquittal of police officers accused of assaulting Rodney King.

Even though he no longer held official responsibilities with the LAPD, Vernon was prepared to assist in quelling the riots. From Florida, he had talked with department officials who asked him to remain on the alert, but he was not summoned. All he could do was view the dramatic TV news coverage of the tragic disruption and looting. The images tore at emotional scar tissue from the preceding twelve months that had not yet fully healed.

First to See Videotape

On May 4, 1991, Vernon was the acting chief of police in Los Angeles while Police Chief Daryl Gates was in Miami attending a conference of major city police chiefs. In that capacity, Vernon became the first police official to learn of the videotape that showed King being clubbed by police officers the night before.

"Our press relations officer called me and said, 'Stan Chambers from Channel 5 has a videotape that will be shown tonight on the ten o'clock news. He thinks you ought to see it. Do you have time to do that?'

"I responded, 'If Stan Chambers thinks I need to see a video, then I need to see it. Go get it.'"

By 4:30 P.M., Vernon was viewing the video of Los Angeles police officers beating King with nightsticks. Within days, the video would be shown across the country and viewed by millions.

Investigation Ordered

"I didn't like what I saw," Vernon states. "I did not know all the facts, but what I saw made me sick to my stomach. I had carried a nightstick for twelve years on street beats before moving into supervision and management, and had only used it twice. Both times were in bar fights where I was outnumbered ten to one and it was the only thing I could do."

He immediately ordered an investigation, starting with gathering up all evidence, including uniforms and nightsticks, seizing all reports related to the incident, and bringing in all the officers involved.

In the weeks that followed, Vernon intentionally distanced himself from the investigation. As assistant police chief, he was often called upon to make public statements and to speak at numerous civic functions. He did not want to have to lie about the case, but at the same time he did not want to release information that could prejudice the trial.

The avalanche of criticism and news reports over the next months, decrying the Los Angeles Police Department as a poorly run, racist, brutal, and sexist organization, cut deeply. *Professionalism* and *dedication* were words that he felt best described the LAPD, not brutality.

His love affair with police work had begun soon after his birth in 1933. His father was a police officer in Los Angeles, and Bob followed suit by joining the force in 1954.

Early Test as a Police Officer

He fondly recalls his first true test as a policeman. He had only been an officer for three weeks when he was advised that an escaped felon from San Quentin Penitentiary was suspected to be on his beat. Vernon's partner had called in sick and, since radio transmitters had not yet been put to use, he would spend the day alone, looking for an escapee who had vowed not to be taken alive.

He found the convict in a seedy bar that afternoon. Nervously approaching the fugitive, Vernon confirmed the suspect's identity and then, with service revolver clutched in his very shaky right hand, ordered the escapee to surrender. Later, the criminal told another officer it was "not fair" to send a rookie policeman to apprehend him. "He was so nervous, I was afraid he was going to shoot!" he said. Vernon comments, "He was probably right."

Throughout the career of more than thirty-seven years, he remained excited about his work, "even the calls at three in the morning to tell me that one of our officers had been shot. I wanted to be there, to make sure he got the best care, and that his wife would be notified in the proper way. I loved leading men, making decisions, and being held accountable for them."

So it was with much regret that he took early retirement from the LAPD in April 1992. Initially, after Gates was pressured into resigning, Vernon had been a candidate to succeed him. City politics, however, quickly entered in.

"One newspaper report said for those who were eager to get rid of Daryl Gates to look at who was standing in the wings—Bob Vernon. Then came a series of false accusations, followed by declarations by the president of the police commission and other city officials that they did not want me to remain in the department," he recalls. "I was getting close to retirement and decided that if I could not have the support of the commission and of key members of the City Council, it would ultimately hurt the men and women who were serving in the streets. Those officers and the community would feel the lack of support, and I knew that one man's career was not that important.

Catastrophic Personal Blow

"So I voluntarily took early retirement. I was greatly saddened by this; it was a catastrophic blow personally," Vernon admits. "I still have dreams about it, believe it or not, a recurring dream that I have to get down to headquarters before midnight to stop my retirement papers. Of course, I can't do that.

"I felt as if I were divorcing a woman I still deeply loved, because I love police work, the LAPD, and working in Los Angeles and its various communities. Severing the ties was a real trauma for me."

Ironically, the recurring dreams also resulted from the death of another dream that Vernon had treasured—one of restoring harmony to a city painfully divided.

"Mine was a dream that I could only have fulfilled as chief of police. There were certain things that I felt would bring healing between the racial groups in Los Angeles and bring about a better climate for mutual problem solving as far as our gang situation is concerned. That dream is now dead; I will never be able to implement it."

How did he survive such a sudden and dramatic change, the loss of a career that had been such a beloved part of his life?

Many people asked Vernon that in the weeks that followed. His answer has steadfastly remained the same.

"My relationship with God has gotten me through this," he asserts. "Without Him, I could not have done it.

Lessons from Psalm 37

"Over the past months, Psalm 37 has become near and dear to me. I was fretting and angry about people falsely accusing me and getting away with it. But as I have read and reread this psalm, four principles jumped out at me.

"The first is, God says, 'Trust Me. In the midst of the tribulation, when the going is especially rough, trust Me even more than you normally do.'

"Next, we are to delight ourselves in the Lord. We may not delight in the situation we find ourselves in, but we still are to delight in Him. My dream has evaporated, but I have found that I *can* delight in the solid rock of who God is, not the quicksand of emotion.

"The third principle is that we are to remain committed to Him, not turning back regardless of what happens.

"Fourth, and perhaps hardest of all, is that we are to 'rest' as it says in Psalm 37:7. We say, 'Now, Lord. Do it now!' But He says, 'Wait.'

"During this very difficult time for me, my wife Esther, and our family, we have seen that God does answer our prayers—but not always as we expect. His answers may be 'No,' 'Not now,' 'Wait,' or simply, 'Endure.'"

While this passage has been an ongoing source of hope and reassurance, the ordeal the Vernons faced never has become easy. As the tempest surrounding the police department and Gates's successor intensified, charges were made that Vernon promoted racism, would not hire homosexuals, discriminated against women, and showed preference to fellow Christians in the department. Each allegation he refuted and no evidence was ever produced to support any of the claims, but they continued to be the subject of heavy media reports.

"Many nights before I officially retired, I would come home and have Esther meet me at the door in tears, asking, 'Do you know what they are saying about you right now?' My grandchildren would see my picture in the papers with some new allegation and wonder why people didn't like me.

Angry with God

"I have to be honest: There have been times when I was angry at God. I know that's wrong and I don't try to justify it, but I'm human and this can happen to any of us. The great thing is I can treat this just like any other sin—confessing it, asking the Lord's forgiveness, and sensing His love and grace."

Another Bible passage that has sustained Vernon during this time of turmoil is Romans 5:1–4, which says that sufferings lead to perseverance, which leads to proven character and then to hope.

"Proven character, to me, means that you become proof that Jesus Christ is real," he says. "A lot of people have been watching me during this time—I know because many of them have told me—so it has been important that in enduring the events of the last year, my life would demonstrate that what I talk about is real."

*Trust in the Lord with all your heart
and lean not on your own understanding;
in all your ways acknowledge him,
and he will make your paths straight.*

—Proverbs 3:5–6

Terminated: Effective Immediately!

*W*e have carried unrealistic expectations about our jobs. We thought losing a job was like being robbed or mugged. "It won't *really* happen to me." No matter how bad the numbers got or how closely the ax fell, deep down we nurtured a mysterious optimism that somehow, maybe through hard work and caution, we would be exempt.

Such optimism may reignite our zeal for our jobs one more day, but it doesn't make mortgage payments. In today's chaotic business environment, as many millions of men and women can attest, losing your job *can* happen to you. In 1991 alone, more than 25 million U.S. workers heard some version of "Terminated: Effective Immediately." For years, corporate America has been dumping management and white-collar workers like excess cargo on high seas.

This section is about how to stay afloat in the high seas—if and when losing a job happens to you. How do you cope with the loss of a job—and what steps do you take when comparable jobs can't be found?

For Christians, it's time to bring "front and center" a truth that has slumbered in the backs of our minds all along: Our loyalties don't belong to a company anyway. Ultimately, God is our employer and He promises to meet our needs. In the absence of a secure job, trust and faith have a way of taking on deeper, more profound meaning. This must at the same time be combined with the 2 Thessalonians 3:10 admonition, "If a man will not work, he shall not eat."

So how should we respond when job loss becomes a personal issue? What difference does Jesus Christ make at such a time?

Chapter 9

Double Whammy

Shutting down my company, and losing another job

Steve Garrison

The recession came late to Southern California, but when it did arrive, it came with full force. The slowdown in commercial real estate started in late 1990, and by the end of the first quarter of the following year, the industry had virtually come to a standstill.

During the two previous years, my company, Garrison Developments, had built thirty-six buildings in five industrial parks, for sale and for lease. Those years were very good for the company financially, but early in 1991 I found myself with nine commercial and industrial buildings remaining for sale—and no buyers.

With all of our assets tied up in the properties, my cash reserves were quickly depleted. My wife Joy and I reluctantly had to cash in our IRAs to meet financial obligations and commitments. In April of 1991 I had no choice but to terminate my last remaining employees and close the doors to Garrison Development.

Coming and Going

While I was taking these painful steps, I had an opportunity to join a commercial real estate consulting firm with several offices around the United States. Even though I'm an entrepreneur at heart, my job as senior account manager came at a crucial time—a true answer to prayer.

I had settled into the new position, and was beginning to enjoy my job when, on September 10, our new regional vice-president called me into his office and told me I was being let go "effective today." With real estate development in a slump across the country, the company was being forced to make cutbacks. And as our office's most recent addition, I was the first to be laid off.

This news took me by complete surprise. I had felt it was a good job; there was no inkling that cutbacks were imminent. My response? To be honest, at first I felt like I had received the double whammy—first having to shut down my company, and then losing another job.

It was a time for digging deeply into my Christian faith, which has served as the foundation of my life for the past eighteen years. Although I didn't like my circumstances, I had to remind myself that I worship a sovereign God, who is absolutely in control of everything that happens in the lives of His people. Therefore, I also had to trust that God will not have me work for a company any longer—or shorter—than He sees fit.

Seeking the Lord's direction, I have found that while outwardly much of my life has been in turmoil, God has used this time to draw me closer to Himself.

For years, my pattern has been to wake up about 5 A.M. for my devotional time. But as the real estate market slowed to a halt, I would awaken at 2 or 3 A.M. with my mind trying to work through my problems—worries about losing my business, my home, how to meet financial obligations, the possibility of bankruptcy, and not being able to provide for my family. Initially, I would try to go back to sleep, but then I determined that rather than worrying about something I could not control, I would get an early start on my quiet time for the day.

These times became wonderful, high-quality, one-on-one times with God. Without a clock pressing at my back, I had the freedom to study the Bible at length, read Christian biographies and even *Foxe's Book of Martyrs*, trying to gain insight from the struggles of great believers from decades and centuries past.

In the process, I discovered some things about myself that I didn't like. For instance, I had always thought that I held my material possessions and professional status very loosely, recognizing them as gifts from God. But as the Lord enabled me to take an honest look at myself, I was dismayed to find that my reputation, the esteem of colleagues, my net worth and assets meant much more to me than I had realized. Jesus spoke about the "deceitfulness of riches" in Mark 4:19 (NASB)—I had not realized how much this applied to me.

Learning True Dependence

Character traits such as these, it seems, have not revealed themselves in me during easier times. For me, true dependence on the Lord wasn't *really* learned until I reached the point where I had no choice but to *be* dependent.

I also recognized that I had been more critical of people and less patient toward them than I had realized. As someone who for more than a year desperately needed to receive grace, I now understand the need to dispense grace more freely to others.

It felt like God was lovingly beating me up—as I believe He is doing with the evangelical church in America in general—seeking our complete, undivided attention. With affluence providing stiff competition, the best way to accomplish this is to remove the affluence. It seems to be working.

Without question, my future has never seemed so uncertain. Prospects for commercial real estate development in Southern California don't look promising, with some experts predicting the trend may not turn around for another five years. Most of us in the business can't wait that long. Joy and I surely are in no position to wait for an extended period of time.

The personal and financial pressures I have experienced are unlike anything I have known before, and I praise the Lord that I haven't succumbed to the adversity. I'm not being dramatic—it's just a reality of the business I have been in for so long.

A friend of mine recently commented that in the 1980s, many of us mistook luck for brains. Business was going so well here that virtually anyone could make a good profit. We are now paying the penalty for too much leverage and too much optimism. None of us was prepared for the downturn. The natural consequences of a highly leveraged business in a cyclical industry have become painfully evident. The wisdom of the biblical exhortations against cosigning for another (such as my corporation) has proved itself in our weakened economy.

Right now, although I have been able to work part-time with a bank as a real estate consultant, I recognize that nothing in this world is permanent. For the first time, I'm having to consider changing careers. As my family continues to struggle financially, we may not be able to keep my daughter, Amy, in the college she has attended for three years. Other lifestyle changes may be necessary as well.

People Are Watching

But another friend pointed out something that humbled me more than a personal financial crisis ever could. For years, I have led businessmen's Bible studies and have personally discipled a number of men. "Steve," my friend said, "a lot of men are looking at you, watching to see if your faith is for real."

In one sense, it's encouraging to think God could use a difficult time like this to demonstrate that my trust in Him is not just rhetoric. But it's also very scary, because I know that if I compromise my faith, a lot of people are going to notice.

Joy has been a great trouper during this entire time. She hasn't complained about having to do much of the paperwork in closing down the business, even though it's something she neither enjoys nor has been trained to do. Our financial situation hasn't been easy, either, but she has been a tremendous support for me.

As a person who loves to tell others about Jesus Christ, I have found our troubled economy to be very helpful. People know that my family and I are hurting, that we are facing tremendous pressures, so they have felt comfortable to come to us with their problems. Recently, three other couples from our industry have been meeting with Joy and me in our home to study what the Bible has to say concerning hard times like these. It's amazing how open they have been to the truths in the Word of God.

After enjoying the benefits of material prosperity, we are learning about another side of God's blessings, discovering how to prosper spiritually in times of adversity. In 1 Peter 4:12–13, it says, "Dear friends, do not be surprised at the painful trial you are suffering, as though something strange were happening to you. But rejoice that you participate in the sufferings of Christ, so that you may be overjoyed when his glory is revealed."

Clinging to the Truth

I'm thankful there has never been a moment when I have felt that God was ignoring me. Joy and I cling to the truth that He knows what we are going through and that He will not fail to meet our needs. God loves His own and promises to care for His children.

We can't say enough about the prayer support and encouragement we have received from friends around the country, particularly those we know through Christian Business Men's Committee, as well as our friends here at home. This has really made a difference in our attitude and response to this very difficult time in our lives.

These experiences have served as a great schoolhouse for me. My prayer, and I mean this reverently, is that I graduate before my time on earth comes to an end. However, while I remain in this "schoolhouse," my goal is to love and trust God, and allow Him to use me in His plans.

Chapter 10

The Agony of Defeat

I was out of a job—effective immediately

Ted Sprague

Most of us remember the opening to TV's "Wide World of Sports": the long-distance runner with arms raised high, signaling "the thrill of victory," and in the next picture, a ski jumper tumbling as he reaches the edge of the ramp, falling in a tangle of arms and legs to "the agony of defeat."

For me, these scenes could depict my career in late 1990 and early 1991. On September 24, 1990, I was part of a contingent of leaders from Atlanta who returned victorious from Tokyo, where our city was awarded the honor of hosting the 1996 Summer Olympics. This capped off an incredible series of achievements for the city—hosting the Democratic National Convention in 1988, and then being selected as the site for the Super Bowl and World Cup soccer matches in 1994. The thrill of victory had become a welcome daily companion.

So I was totally unprepared for the turn of events on February 20, 1991. Since that day marks the birthday of my wife, Tudi, it is normally a happy day. And when I walked into a meeting with my chairman, my past chairman, and the chairman-elect, I was overflowing with confidence and enthusiasm. I had compiled what I felt was an impressive package of marketing plan adjustments for the year and couldn't wait to unveil them. But I never got the chance.

The chairman said, "Ted, we would like to talk to you." "Sure," I replied. "About what?" He answered, "We're not going to renew your contract."

That was it. No preliminaries, no warning. Despite having just completed my most successful year out of twenty-five in the convention and tourism business, I found myself out of a job— effective immediately.

Fired as a Champion

If I had been a pro football coach and had just finished a 3-13 season, I would not have been surprised. But 1990 for me had been my industry's equivalent of a 15-1 season, plus a victory in the Super Bowl. Normally, I don't have trouble expressing my thoughts, but all I could say upon being informed that my contract was being terminated was, "Wow!" I did quickly think of something else to say: "Unbelievable."

Without further discussion, I was excused from the office. As I was leaving the building, chairmen past, present, and future were firing four senior executives, and then reducing the remaining employees by 20 percent, even though 1990 had been a very profitable year.

Driving home, I called my wife on the car phone. "Tudi, I'm coming home," I told her. "Because of my birthday?" she asked. "How romantic!"

"Honey, are you sitting down?" "No," she answered. "Please, sit." I explained to her that, even as we spoke, a press conference was being held to announce my dismissal. Like me, Tudi suddenly became a person of few words. "What?" was all she could say.

How to Respond?

My job wasn't terminated for any wrongdoing. The reasons are not important at this point. What is important is how one responds if such a thing occurs. Whether you are in a very public, high profile position as I, or at the low end of the seniority scale, losing your job is a shock. And it can be a crushing blow if you don't have the right resources for such a crisis.

For Tudi and me, it was our unwavering faith in a loving, sovereign God that carried us through—and continues to do so today. And I was thankful that, twenty-six years before, the Lord had impressed upon me the importance of spending time in His Word every day. My Christian faith had grown to the point where even losing a job I had loved for the past nine years could not shake my confidence in a God who knew me before the beginning of time and who had promised never to leave me or forsake me.

When I arrived home, Tudi and I went for a walk. I prayed, asking for wisdom in what to say to my wife who was already deeply burdened by the ongoing illness of Trisha, our twenty-one-year-old daughter. Trisha had been suffering for four months with diabetic gastroperesis, a disease that shuts down the stomach. At the time of my firing, her weight had dropped to ninety-eight pounds and she was in daily agony. (We are thankful that today, after more than a year, she is improving slowly but steadily, anticipating her return to college.)

Comfort from Job

As we walked, I sought to comfort Tudi from what the Lord had taught me through the Scriptures. Instead of the familiar passages of comfort, my thoughts went to the Book of Job, where in the second chapter, after suffering many personal losses and physical affliction, Job asks his wife, "Shall we accept good from God, and not trouble?" (2:10).

I don't want to sound self-righteous, because I was as dumb-founded as anyone who has lost his job unexpectedly. But I couldn't help thinking about how gracious God had been to us over the years and knew this was no time to start doubting Him. "Who do I think I am that this would never happen to me?" I asked Tudi. "Who do I think I am?"

No More Security

We used to think security came from seniority on an assembly line, or tenure at a university, or a sense of being "indispensable" at work. But in recent years, many of us have found there is no such thing as job security—even in the most secure jobs.

We all like victory, whether it's on the playing field or in the boardroom. It's a lot more fun to talk about than defeat. But in reality, we know that life is a mix—win some, lose some. Before I got into the convention and tourism industry, I attended college on a baseball scholarship and played in semipro and professional rookie leagues. Often I have thought back to those days, realizing that life, too, is a game of hardball. Sometimes you hit a home run, sometimes you strike out. We don't always know what life will bring.

As Tudi and I worked through the initial shock of my firing, I began to consider my next steps. For two weeks, I thought about calling a major press conference. I felt I had been treated unfairly and wanted to tell my side of the story. Many of my mature Christian friends even agreed. But every time I read the Word of God, He kept telling me, "Endure, Ted. Persevere, Ted. Have patience, Ted. Be mature, Ted."

Vengeance Is God's

So my press conference was never called. If there was a wrong to be righted, that was God's responsibility, not mine. The Lord burned the words of 1 Peter 3:14, 17 into my heart: "But even if you should suffer for what is right, you are blessed. . . . It is better, if it is God's will, to suffer for doing good than for doing evil." And in Romans 12:14, 19, it says, "Bless those who persecute you; bless and do not curse. . . .'It is mine to avenge; I will repay,' says the Lord." God's ways, I have learned, are best.

My mind later turned to Joseph, a godly man who walked through many undeserved trials. He endured those trials with incredible faith and unwavering confidence. I knew the Lord was asking me, and Tudi, to do the same as we dealt with both my job loss and Trisha's lingering illness.

Hidden Blessing

Physically, my daughter's health has not been a blessing, but spiritually it has. During this period, she latched onto Psalm 75:3 as her favorite verse. It says, "When the earth and all its people quake, it is I [the Lord] who hold its pillars firm." In one Bible edition, a footnote on this verse reads, "when everything is falling apart around you, God has everything under control." As it says in Hebrews 12:28, "Therefore, since we are receiving a kingdom that cannot be shaken, let us be thankful, and so worship God acceptably with reverence and awe."

At this writing, my vocational future remains uncertain. I am considering other similar tourism positions, but I'm not sure that God wants us to leave Atlanta. He has blessed us with many ministry opportunities, and I'm reluctant to leave those behind. So for the present, I have started a convention and tourism consulting business to cities throughout the world. How successful it will be remains an unknown, but I am very excited about giving it a diligent try.

Victory Is Forever

I have known the thrill of victory; I have also felt the agony of defeat. But knowing my life is secure in Christ, I have the confidence that while defeat is temporary, victory is literally forever.

Our trials can prove to be blessings as they build godly character in us and show our faith to be genuine. As the Book of Job points out, we may not know why we go through trials— and we don't have to know. The key is learning to acknowledge God's sovereignty in our circumstances and getting to know Him better in the process.

Although I don't know exactly what the future holds for me and my family, God's Word in 2 Corinthians 1 tells me that a result of my trials and the comfort the Lord has given will be the opportunity to comfort others enduring similar circumstances. This I have adopted as a new goal. Through God's design, the loss of health and loss of a job have actually given me a greater purpose for living!

How to Help a Friend

While nearly 20 percent of all Americans have experienced joblessness during the past year, the remainder of us have succeeded in remaining gainfully employed. For us, the question might be, "How can I assist friends who are out of work in a meaningful way?" Here are just some ideas to consider (which hopefully will trigger more):

▲ Buy the unemployed family gift certificates to a local grocery store.

▲ Call frequently to encourage and pray with them.

▲ Help them to "network" with people who might offer leads for possible jobs.

▲ Buy a gift certificate to a restaurant and offer to baby-sit so mom and dad can enjoy an evening out.

▲ Offer to take the unemployed couple's child when your family does ordinary things, such as skating or grabbing a quick bite at McDonald's.

▲ Loan your children's outgrown clothing to their children (appropriate size and season, of course).

▲ Provide transportation so the couple can limit use of their own car.

▲ Take the family out to lunch and on other fun, free outings with your own family.

▲ Take them a bag of essential groceries.

▲ Call to let them know of any job possibilities.

▲ Make sure their cars are in running order.

▲ Give cash, perhaps even anonymously. The bills don't stop when the paycheck does.

▲ Quietly listen to their concerns, worries, fears, and doubts without being judgmental.

At Christmas or other special holidays:

▲ Supply the ingredients needed for special holiday baking.

▲ Give gifts and stocking stuffers for the children.

▲ Provide something special (not a necessity) for the husband to give to his wife (and vice versa).

▲ Give money for husband and wife to buy each other a gift.

▲ Most of all, as one couple that has benefited from some of these forms of help advised: pray, pray, pray.

(These suggestions courtesy of Mark and Luanne Kessel of Chattanooga, Tennessee, who have experienced the trials of unemployment firsthand.)

Chapter 11

Which Way to Turn?

Losing a job can become a positive career move

Jack Davies

Outplacement. It may sound like some bureaucratic term for being "put out to pasture," but in 1986 my job was eliminated, and outplacement came to mean "new lease on life" to me.

I had been with the company for eight years, and as part of my severance package, they included the services of an outplacement firm. At first, I didn't even know what "outplacement" meant. To my surprise, I discovered it represented a whole philosophy for helping people who are out of work make a positive career move.

As I began the process, I was encouraged to take a step back and reevaluate my vocational course, rather than rush to grab the first available job.

Through a series of surveys and self-evaluation exercises, as well as input from my wife, Caroline, I learned how to pinpoint my "motivated strengths"—those areas where my abilities and personal interests overlap.

The purpose was to either confirm that I was well-suited for the kind of work I had been doing, or reveal other areas where I was more likely to excel and find fulfillment by linking my abilities and interests to best advantage.

Lessons in Networking

The outplacement firm taught me about networking—utilizing already established contacts, not only professionally, but also through church, other organizations, hobbies, and other areas of common interest—to gain advice and referrals in the process of investigating alternative career options.

Being let go was a traumatic experience for me. A large part of my identity involved the work I did. When I lost my job, my self-esteem and self-worth also suffered. I had to cling to biblical promises like Jeremiah 29:11, "'For I know the plans I have for you,' declares the Lord, 'plans to prosper you and not to harm you, plans to give you hope and a future.'"

Focusing on Strengths

Losing my job actually was a blessing, although Caroline saw that more quickly than I did. Some aspects of my job had not been satisfying, but I liked the "security." The outplacement evaluation helped me discover that managing operational details—a big part of my previous job—was not one of my strengths. As group new products manager in a grocery products company, I had been much better in developing marketing strategies and working in face-to-face or small-group settings.

Helping people turned out to be one of my primary motivated strengths. Ironically, as I proceeded through the outplacement process, I saw that type of work as something I might really enjoy. Although the name of the firm was Right Associates, the timing wasn't right for me.

After about eight months, I accepted a position as director of marketing for a regional sausage processing company. The job went well, and I was able to implement much of what I had learned during outplacement. But I still felt a desire to work with other people who were facing job transitions.

I initiated a networking meeting with the new managing principal of the Right Associates' Baltimore office. This led to my being hired in the summer of 1989 to replace another person who had been promoted. Since then, this has been an ideal job for me.

Having gone through the same type of struggle, I can easily empathize with people whose jobs have been terminated, phased out, or eliminated for a variety of reasons. I also can draw on my varied business background and marketing experiences to help people market themselves.

Great Anxiety

Losing a job can cause a lot of anxiety, ranging from struggling with the rationale for leaving the company to embarrassment over not being employed. It affects feelings of belonging and purpose. But as I have learned through personal experience, God can turn a hurtful and worrisome situation into a source of joy and renewed enthusiasm.

One example that comes to mind is a fifty-seven-year-old man I met. He had worked for one company all his adult life—probably thirty-five years or more. The company did give him a generous severance package, including our outplacement services. His first question to me was, "Do you think anybody would want to hire me at fifty-seven?"

About four months into the process, the man found a job with a smaller company doing something he loved and did very well. And since the severance pay overlapped compensation at his new job for a number of months, he was able to use the added income as he desired. At the age of fifty-seven, he was replacing a man who had just retired at the age of eighty! So I suggested to him that in his new job, he might be able to work twenty-three more years before retiring!

Special Satisfaction

As a Christian, I find great satisfaction in helping people discover God-given abilities and talents so they can use them to the fullest. Our company employs and works with people from all backgrounds and beliefs, so I'm not going to counsel someone with a Right Associates manual in one hand and a Bible in the other. But my boss knows of my commitment to Jesus Christ, and on several occasions has assigned me to work with people who have indicated a spiritual inclination early on in the process.

Colossians 3:23 tells us that whatever we do, we should do it for the Lord, rather than for men. So it makes good sense to determine what kind of work God has uniquely designed us to perform, and then find the right place to put those abilities to work.

In Proverbs 3:5–6, we are urged to "Trust in the Lord with all your heart and lean not on your own understanding; in all your ways acknowledge him, and he will make your paths straight." If my job had not been done away with in 1986, I probably wouldn't be doing outplacement counseling today, the most fulfilling work I have ever done.

Advice for Job Hunters: Evaluate Strengths, Weigh Your Options

Jack Davies offers the following counsel for those who are out of work or desire to find a new job:

Process

"Realize that you're in a process. Regard this as a unique opportunity to reexamine your career course that you probably would not have taken otherwise."

Strengths

"Focus on your motivated strengths—those areas where you are uniquely gifted or talented."

Career Steps

"Remember, you're not looking for just a job, but your best next career step. Talk with people to benefit from their advice and gain referrals to other people as you investigate and focus on appropriate career options. Building a network of contacts within your career area can be the key."

Transition

"Today, there is no stigma to being 'in transition.' With all the company downsizings and closings, there are many people temporarily out of work. Don't let pride get in the way of letting people know you're in the middle of a career change. Even a social party can be the source of eight to ten good contacts that could lead to job possibilities."

What's Happening

"Introverts often do as well as extroverts in this process. People appreciate knowing what's happening in your life, and 90 percent of them would love to be of help."

Emotional Rollercoaster

"Be aware that looking for a new job can put you on a huge emotional rollercoaster. You can have a good interview and feel way up, but if you don't receive a call, your emotions can drop way down. Find people to support and encourage you, people who are willing to serve as sounding boards on anything and everything."

Chapter 12

Three Steps to Landing a Job

Strategy, homework, and perseverance

Victor Coppola

Looking for a job today is a marketing and sales campaign. That's the assessment of Victor Coppola, partner-in-charge of the emerging business services group for Coopers & Lybrand in Philadelphia.

Coppola regularly receives résumés and phone calls from men and women requesting assistance in finding jobs. Today more than ever, with downsizings and mergers, even being considered for a job requires more than simply contacting the right person and declaring your availability.

/ / /

If you want to get someone's attention, you need to do three things: develop a strategy, do your homework, and stay at it.

Strategy

Rather than shotgunning résumés around the country at random—according to some reports only 10 percent, and sometimes as low as 1 percent, are even acknowledged—it would be wise to research prospective companies, learn about the types of work they do, and then evaluate how your own background could benefit them.

I receive loads of résumés, but in most cases, people don't take the time to customize their cover letters to relate to a company's situation and needs. It behooves the job seeker to get as much information as possible so he can demonstrate how his skills and experiences can match what the business is looking for.

Homework

This information gathering could include talking with current employees or networking with others who have contact with the company, reading annual reports, going to a library to find news articles about the firm, and requesting some of the company's promotional, sales, or recruiting brochures.

People who do their homework in any area of business are the ones who excel, and it's true in looking for a job. Homework always impresses the reader—it's a way to distinguish yourself from the rest of the pack.

Perseverance

An old adage, "persistence neutralizes resistance," applies to trying to find a new job, according to a twenty-seven-year veteran of the accounting industry. Courteous but constant networking is appropriate. If you make contact once every thirty to forty-five days, you're not being a pest. It shows you are still interested, and gives you an opportunity to tell your contact person what you have been doing that might enhance your chances for consideration.

When you land a job, send a note to inform those people you had been contacting regularly. It shows you appreciated their time and interest. You never know when you might be in the job market again.

Chapter 13

Taking Action

One man's response to the loss of a job

Patrick O'Neal

Losing a job is never pleasant, but having no cash reserves—and no severance provisions—compounds the problem.

Patrick and Tina O'Neal faced this dilemma after Pat was fired by the new sales manager of a prestigious residential development company in Chapel Hill, North Carolina, even though Pat had been the top-producing salesperson.

/ / /

In July of 1989 we had moved to the Chapel Hill area from Hilton Head, South Carolina, after being offered a relocation opportunity by my employer. We visited the area and liked it very much, but more importantly, found there had been two men meeting for several years praying to get a Christian Business Men's Committee started. This confirmed our decision to move.

When we moved to North Carolina, I once again claimed the first Bible verse I ever memorized, Proverbs 3:5–6, "Trust in the Lord with all your heart, and lean not on your own understanding; in all your ways acknowledge Him, and He shall direct your paths" (NKJV).

We knew with the relocation it would take about two years to build a client and owner base to be financially successful in the project. However, God had blessed us, and 1990 had gone better than expected.

Then came March 2, 1991. Pat and the other salesmen had just completed a two-week kick-off campaign for what was expected to be the beginning of two highly productive years of sales.

I fully expected my many months of hard work to really pay off, projecting my sales commissions for 1991 to be between $150,000 and $180,000. But, without notice, I was fired. There was no previous mention that my employers had been unhappy with me. And they offered no severance pay. Tina and I didn't have a nest egg, so immediately we were in a financial bind.

Pat's first responses were shock and anger. But he quickly realized there was no time for self-pity; he had to find another job. Asking "why" and wondering "if only" would not pay the bills.

We liked the Durham area and our kids were in a great school, so we didn't want to look for a job in another city. Having been a Christian for nearly fourteen years, I began to pray for wisdom and direction. Once again, I was trusting in Proverbs 3:5–6, with great fervency. I was very grateful to have my CBMC prayer group for encouragement, support, and counsel.

Within a week, Pat had two business ideas, applying his diversified background in real estate sales, marketing, and development. The first was a real estate brokerage service that could take specifications from prospective land buyers and find properties that matched their needs. This approach has been successful on the West Coast, according to Pat.

The second idea adapted a concept from commercial construction management to custom homes. Since Pat has experience in home building as well as sales, he envisioned serving as a liaison between the property owner and the architects, lenders, and builders, assisting lot owners with the complexities of planning a new home and finding ways to reduce costs without cutting quality.

Ideas Need Resources

Good ideas often come more easily than resources to carry them out. So Pat sought counsel from five Christian friends in business. He explained the buyers' building service concept and asked them to "shoot holes in it." All responded positively to the consumer having a personal advocate in dealing with developers, salespeople, and builders.

But how do you start a new business with no capital? The O'Neals owned both their automobiles, so they used the cars as collateral to obtain a small business loan and enough money to meet their immediate personal financial needs.

Pat's first step in business was presenting his new service to about three hundred people who owned property in the development where he used to work. This mailing yielded his first client—to whom he had previously sold a patio lot.

After six weeks, Pat reconvened his five Christian advisers from the CBMC group, updated them on the business, and again asked for recommendations. They affirmed he seemed headed in the right direction, even though the business remained far from profitable.

Help from Friends

After the meeting, one friend offered to loan Pat money from a maturing CD to help cover operating costs of the business during the start-up phase.

It was overwhelming to see God provide for our needs through this brother and sister in Christ. It would have been impossible to sustain the business without their help.

Commissions from lot sales through his residential brokerage service, The Real Estate Company, have provided some income while the other company, Buyers Building Service, Inc., builds recognition and clients.

People are seeing the advantages of having someone else handle the headaches of getting a house built right, for a price they can afford. Some builders don't like the idea, because it requires an accountability they're not accustomed to, but for others, it simplifies life. They don't have to deal day to day with the homeowners.

Forced to Use Talents

Although he remembers the sting of being fired, Pat sees the Lord's direction in the entire process.

If I really consider the talents that God has given me, what I'm good at and what I enjoy, I can't think of anything that I could enjoy more. Even with the financial pressures, this has been the happiest I have been in years.

Tina, who is an interior designer, has been able to assist Pat in space planning and decorating needs.

It's really been a blessing—the silver lining inside what I saw as a dark cloud. God is so faithful, but I have to constantly remember what He has already done for us in the past to appreciate what He is doing in the present.

When I was fired, it was difficult to see how God would use the situation for His glory. Circumstances, obviously, weren't pleasant in our lives, but we continued to trust that God is in control and working to accomplish His ultimate good for everyone involved.

Our business continues to grow, and we are getting great opportunities to tell our new clients about Christ. Financially, things are still very tight, but we try to remember that in Proverbs 13:11 God says things are built "little by little."

Therefore be careful how you walk,
not as unwise men, but as wise,
making the most of your time,
because the days are evil.

—Ephesians 5:15–16, NASB

The Time Trap

When hours are no longer ours

Let's face it: Time really can't be managed. It passes whether we like it or not. Each twenty-four hours moves at a twenty-four-hour rate, minute by minute, hour by hour. We can't retrieve yesterday; tomorrow is always a day away.

So why try to manage the unmanageable? First, despite the inability to stem time's passing, we can exert some control over how our time is used. Second, the Bible admonishes us to "walk circumspectly, not as fools but as wise, redeeming the time" (Eph. 5:15–16, NKJV). Other versions translate this "making the most of your time" (NASB) or "making the most of every opportunity" (NIV).

Time is precious simply because it cannot be saved or re-trieved. Once past, it's gone forever. But time also is sacred: God entrusts it to each of us, rationed out daily. We may have different talents and varied resources, but we all have only two dozen hours per day, sixty minutes per hour, sixty seconds per minute.

How we utilize every one of these moments comprises what we term "time management."

One study calculated that during a seventy-year lifespan, a typical person sleeps twenty-three years, works sixteen years, watches eight years of TV, eats and travels six years *each*, devotes four and a half years to leisure—and two years to dressing! Spiritual pursuits? Six months.

While not one of us is "typical," it's amazing—and sometimes distressing—how our time is spent (or squandered). As Christians, we may wonder how to approach the matter of time management from a biblical perspective. Should it differ from the approach of people who do not share a commitment to Jesus Christ? If so, how—and why? For instance, how would a Christian banker, stockbroker, and account executive structure the workday differently from an equally dedicated, but non-Christian counterpart? Must every hour be accounted for? Does Christ want inflexible followers who structure their days by clock and calendar? And what about interruptions—is there a "Christian" way to handle them?

Chapter 14

Digging Out from Overloaded Days

Making the most of your time

Bob Shank

Members of the Baby Boom generation wear many labels; one of the least desirable, but most applicable, is the one marked "frustrated." Today, we are experiencing more and enjoying it less.

Mention time management to a "boomer" and you'll get a check for $39.95 as payment in full for the course. We are scouring the marketplace for tapes, tips, and tricks to install more into our already overloaded days. If the present activity level doesn't satisfy, will an increase in frenetic activity solve the problem?

More than ineffective *time* management, our problem may be in the area of *life* management. If you aren't sure you are doing the right things, doing more of the wrong things won't help. You see, well-managed days do not result in a well-managed life. Well-managed days *are the result of* a well-managed life!

The first step in honing your life management is a reconfirmation of your primary life mission. In Mark 13:34, Jesus says that each of His servants has a unique assignment in life ("each with his assigned task"). Are you fully aware of yours?

Before endeavoring to become more efficient, it is imperative to examine ways to become more effective. The two are not the same. Unless you are clear about what you are trying to achieve in a lifetime, how can you know what you should accomplish in the course of a day?

Once your mission has been clarified, there are some great principles for managing your time that are modeled in the most effective life in history, during the three years of Jesus' public ministry. Here are four tips on time management we can glean from the life of Christ:

1. *Understand the difference between an agenda and a schedule.* It's possible to fall into the trap of becoming a servant to your schedule and wind up packing it all in but missing the mark. Have you ever passed up an important, unplanned opportunity because you were already booked into another appointment? You may be bypassing the most significant openings because of your allegiance to your day planner.

Jesus had a constant sense of His agenda, His purpose on earth. In Luke 19:10, He expressed it concisely: "For the Son of Man came to seek and to save what was lost." It was to this that He directed His time and energy.

Your *agenda* is a clear statement of what you are trying to accomplish, whether in a single day or in a lifetime. Your *schedule* is an order of events as they are expected to occur. When your schedule reflects your agenda, you are in good shape. When an unplanned chance to advance your agenda conflicts with your schedule, let it supersede. You will increase effectiveness; it is worth the cost of reshuffling.

2. *Invest your time as seriously as you do your money.* Most people would never be as loose with their money as they tend to be with their time. If you are frugal with your finances, you

should be doubly so with your days! You can always get more money, but you'll never increase your access to hours.

This is one case where being polite can be counterproductive. The fact that someone has your phone number and a quarter does not give them the right to fifteen minutes of your life. A phone message is not an obligation; God does not condemn people for not returning superfluous phone calls immediately.

We see an example of this attitude in Jesus' life in the eleventh chapter of the Gospel of John. When the messenger came to tell Him that Lazarus was sick, Jesus did not drop what He was doing and rush to Bethany. In fact, He waited two more days before leaving for Lazarus's hometown, remaining faithful to His plan rather than reacting immediately to the urgent demands of others.

Examine any week in your calendar: Who called the shots? Was your time spent responding or initiating? Were your days invested in your agenda or in the agenda of others? Who called the meeting? Why did you go?

3. Evaluate your portfolio of relationships and focus on the performers. Many hours are poured down the rathole of high-maintenance people who do not offer a return on the investment. Have you suffered the loss of time squandered on men and women who do not show a profit?

Some might call this harsh, but even Jesus was selective about the ones into whom He would invest His limited time. He got to know the crowd, then chose twelve who were high-yield individuals who would give Him a significant return.

Don't spend large amounts of time with people on whom you will not leave an imprint. While it often takes a while to spot the difference between the high-yield and the high-maintenance individuals, once you see their tendencies, it is appropriate to react accordingly.

4. Pursue freedom, if necessary, at the expense of success. One of the greatest delusions of modern society is that freedom is a by-product of success. Ask the movie actor whose widespread recognition prohibits a casual dinner in a public restaurant; ask the corporate executive who can't break away for a two-week vacation with his family because of the high-level negotiations that require his personal attention. Success and freedom can be mutually exclusive—if you could have only one, which would it be?

Without question, Jesus could have spent His time on earth in a high-ranking political office or as a prospering businessman. From a materialistic standpoint, His life was hardly a success. But as we read in Mark 10:45, "the Son of Man did not come to be served, but to serve, and to give his life as a ransom for many."

The Lord did not call attention to Himself, choosing to be as inconspicuous as possible for as long as possible. And when the crush of the crowds became too great, He would withdraw, preferring solitude to celebrity. Then, Jesus performed the ultimate act of freedom, surrendering to death on the cross—failure, as His accusers saw it—to offer forgiveness and life eternal to all who would receive Him.

Many successful people are incapable of conceiving a purpose for their lives. They have become subservient to the advancement of their corporation's agenda and have renounced their freedom in return for the corner office. Are they the winners—or the losers?

Effective time management opens the door for many people in the executive suite, only to find that their precision and order have placed them in a gilded box from which there is no escape. For others, the ability to manage their time has enhanced their flexibility to pursue the variety of high-priority activities that round out their lives and increase the quality-quotient of their days.

The new carrot on the stick for the 1990s is the lure of the simpler life. How will the frenzied professionals of the 1980s achieve this new reward?

It's through the wise investment of time—the great equalizer—that the poster kids of the final decade of the twentieth century will achieve their dreams of a well-ordered life, filled with meaningful, complementary pursuits that color one's palette with richness and destiny. Is it worth going through the motions for less?

Chapter 15

Feeling Covered Up?

Ten businessmen offer tips for managing your time

Approaches to time management are as individualized as the people who use them. For some, the key is finding a compatible method or tool. For others, it is more a matter of why time is to be used, rather than how.

Perhaps you need some ideas on how to better utilize your time each day. Or maybe you feel you're doing fairly well, but wouldn't mind seeing how other people tackle the time management dilemma. The following is a sampling of how some Christian business and professional men across America go about the tricky business of managing time:

One Day at a Time

Time use and goal setting go hand in hand for **Dan Baker**, a senior systems engineer in Pittsburgh, Pennsylvania. "I try to set goals for each day. I've found that going beyond a day is not even realistic for me."

Another tip he has found is not always responding immediately when approached. "Sometimes, if I don't answer questions right away, people will find answers on their own. But if they find they can always get answers from you, there will be no end to the interruptions."

A Clean Desk

Vic Coppola, a partner in a Philadelphia, Pennsylvania, accounting firm, says a clean desk is crucial for his effective time management.

"Keeping my desk clean keeps my focus on doing one thing at a time until it is completed," he said. "Making a list of projects and prioritizing them is helpful, but for me, working on one project until it is done is most effective. I have taken lots of time management courses, but someone who literally forced me to deal with one piece of paper helped me the most. I used to be a 'pile-maker.' There are four things you can do with a piece of paper: handle it, file it, delegate it to someone else, or discard it. When I work on one piece of paper at a time, I have fewer distractions and get more done more quickly."

Take Time to Plan

A daily planning and scheduling tool is helpful, but only if time is allotted to think through that plan, according to **Mike Connor,** director of client services for a health information consulting firm in Ann Arbor, Michigan.

"It's important that you're never too busy to plan the day that lies before you," Connor said. "For me, that planning usually takes place the day before, although I review it at the start of each day. Another thing I try to do is spend time on the highest priorities, although it is tempting to work on lower priority items because they are easier or more fun to do."

First Things First

Tom Clark, president of a real estate consulting firm in Atlanta, Georgia, agrees with the need to establish priorities.

"To manage my time effectively, I have to prioritize the order in which things have to get done. I proceed with top-priority items first, and the items that don't get accomplished are carried over to the next day. Sometimes I find that things that seemed urgent or important really didn't have to be done after all. That way, I don't spend time doing unnecessary work. A lot of stuff cleans itself up."

Acknowledge Your Limits

Perhaps the best way of managing time is acknowledging that humanly, it can't be done. That's the view of **John Endlich** of Vienna, Virginia, director of the financial auditing division in the Office of the Inspector General of the U. S. Department of Energy.

"The only way I can successfully manage my time is to sit down, admit that I can't, and pray, 'Lord, my life is yours.' Then I ask *His* help in planning my day.

"I can't do this just in the morning, either. At the end of the day, the last fifteen minutes at work, I ask God to help me evaluate what I did, where I made mistakes, so I can better understand what I need to do the following day.

"During the evening, I pray about what the Lord has in mind for me tomorrow, and then pray about those plans the next morning. As I pray, I try to make what we used to call 'Kentucky wind adjustments.' I find that as I seek to be faithful to change my plans to meet God's, He greatly blesses me."

Personal Accountability

Putting plans in writing has the effect of maintaining personal accountability for **John Bird**, a regional sales executive with Chrysler Motor Company in Cincinnati, Ohio.

"I use a pocket daily planner for business appointments. To monitor my spiritual development, every day I use a personal spiritual management chart published by Equipping the Saints," Bird said.

"The simple matter of writing goals and accomplishments down helps me to keep on track with the things I need to do. The spiritual management chart, combined with a daily Bible reading guide, help provide the daily discipline to do the things I need to be doing."

What's Important?

Fred Kilgore, an attorney in York, Pennsylvania, concentrates on what's important, rather than a system for scheduling the entire day.

"I try to spend as much time as I can thinking about the important things that should motivate me during the day. I commit my time to the Lord, ask *Him* to prioritize it—rather than me—and I find that He enables me to accomplish what I should be doing that day, although that may differ from what I thought I would be doing.

"It's hard sometimes, but I work to keep unimportant things from monopolizing my time. God does a lot better job of sorting those out than I do."

Limit Goals & Objectives

For **Kevin Ring,** a real estate developer in Walnut Creek, California, a key to time management is restricting written goals and objectives to a workable number. At the start of each week, Ring writes specific objectives he hopes to accomplish in the spiritual, family, physical fitness, and work areas of his life. Then daily he lists items he intends to get done.

"I try not to write down more than five items," he said, recognizing more items probably will not be achieved anyway.

Keep Your Spouse Informed

Without a quiet time to help in ordering the day, life is like launching a missile without setting coordinates, according to **Jonathan Holljes,** a financial consultant in Richmond, Virginia. "If there are no coordinates, the missile will take off, fly around until it runs out of fuel, then land who knows where."

Equally essential in managing his time, Holljes says, is making sure his wife is aware of his plans.

"Many men fail to let their wives know what they are up to. My wife, Jenny, left a good job to become a full-time homemaker. There is nothing more offensive to her than my failure to let her know if I'll be late for dinner.

"Sometimes there's something big on my agenda that I want her to be praying for, and of course, if I make a commitment involving her, it's wise to let her know so she can put it on her calendar. After all, her time is as important as mine."

A Philosophical Approach

It is a philosophy rather than a method that is most important in **Mike Marker's** time management scheme.

Marker, a property manager and real estate developer in Cincinnati, Ohio, said since becoming a Christian, "I have tried to set priorities as to where I'm going to be and when. For instance, it has been almost sacred for me to be home for dinner each night, unless I'm traveling. To do that, I make a conscious decision that my family is more important than any work I'm doing."

Discipling other men, showing them how to study and understand the Bible, has also been a high priority for Marker. Since he generally meets with them on weekday mornings, 7:30 A.M. business meetings are another taboo.

"Fixing these priorities forces me to make better use of my time, focusing on the important rather than the urgent."

Chapter 16

The One Minute Manager

An interview with Kenneth Blanchard

Robert J. Tamasy

Over the past decade, Kenneth Blanchard and The One Minute Manager *have become synonymous. When Blanchard and Spencer Johnson collaborated on the original* One Minute Manager *in 1982, they could not have anticipated its phenomenal success.*

Seven million copies and five sequels later, Blanchard continues to champion this simple approach to management based on people-centered principles. His book, The One Minute Manager Builds High Performing Teams *(1990, with Donald Carew and Eunice Parisi-Carew), extends the one minute manager concept to group dynamics and team building.*

Blanchard is the chairman of Blanchard Training and Development, Inc., in Escondido, California, which conducts training seminars, produces tapes and other training materials, and consults to companies nationwide.

The final word has not been written on the one minute manager, as its creator is working with Gordon MacDonald on a book which will show similarities between Jesus' approach to leadership and the principles of one minute management.

Blanchard discusses the one minute manager's staying power and how this approach relates to managing both people and time.

/ / /

How would you define a one minute manager?

It's a fundamental approach to managing people. The first secret is "One Minute Goal Setting." All good performances start with clear goals. If you don't know where you're going, any road will get you there. So often, as managers or parents, we set goals *after* we get what we don't want.

Once you have set clear goals, you need to see if you can catch your people doing anything right. Then you can give them a pat on the back, what we call a "One Minute Praising"—our second secret. What we typically have done best is catch people doing things wrong.

The third secret is the "One Minute Reprimand." If you are clear on goals and somebody doesn't do it (or doesn't do it right), in the beginning you redirect them—go back to goal setting and seek to clarify what is expected. If they still don't meet goals, even though they have the skills, then you can reprimand them, being as specific as possible about what they did wrong, and expressing your feelings about their performance.

The most important part of the reprimand, however, is a reaffirmation, stating you know the person is better than what he or she has demonstrated. That's why a reprimand is reserved for people with the skills to do the job; it is not appropriate for learners. Reprimands are for "won't do" problems, which are attitudinal. Redirecting is for "can't do" problems, which relate to ability. You can't reprimand people into skills.

Is the one minute manager concept as well-received today as it was when it first came out?

Probably even more, because 1982 was the beginning of even recognizing that without people we aren't going to be able to do much. In the late 1970s and early 1980s, we acted as if the sole purpose of business was to make money. We forgot that if we take care of our people, they will take care of our customers. We lost the loyalty of the work force in a big way in the last ten years, so I think people now see the need for this more than ever. Our book company can't believe it's still selling an average of twenty thousand copies a month of *The One Minute Manager.*

To what extent is this approach general management and leadership, as opposed to time management?

A major time-waster is mismanaging people. Our tendency is to manage people with a ready-fire-aim philosophy, rather than ready-aim-fire. When everybody gets upset, we try to fix it after the fact. If people would manage as we suggest, they would be amazed at how much free time they had.

Time management, as we point out in *The One-Minute Manager Meets the Monkey,* doesn't mean anything if you don't have discretionary time. There are tremendous implications for time management—it's amazing that in most time management programs, mismanaging people is not recognized as a time-waster. If somebody decides to quit and everybody is running around, wondering what went wrong, a lot of time is consumed.

The "monkey" concept in The One Minute Manager Meets the Monkey *is an interesting one. Explain what this term means and its impact on a manager's ability to control the use of his time.*

The analogy is (coauthor) Bill Oncken's, which he developed thirty years ago. The "monkey" stands for the next move that is required to continue a project. What Bill was saying is that problems—or monkeys—you deal with as a manager come from three sources: your boss, your peers, and your people.

When someone comes to me and says, "Ken, we have a problem," I need to be careful because the monkey is about to leap—from the other person's shoulders onto mine. If your boss gives you the monkey, it's more difficult to bat it back to him. If a customer calls and say he's not being treated well, you can't tell him to care for and feed his own monkey. That leaves your people.

Managers with their ego in the wrong place think that when a subordinate brings them a problem, it's because they want to watch expertise in action. But what they are doing is building dependence, rather than independence, and taking away people's opportunity to build their self-esteem.

The monkey concept is very powerful because it can save a significant amount of time if you let the people who already have jobs actually do them.

It seems that proper delegation is crucial here. What is the key to delegating tasks most effectively?

There is a difference between assigning and delegating. In assigning, you are only giving one or two next moves. Delegating could mean giving an entire project to someone. That's a bigger deal, because people have to be able and equipped to follow through with what has been delegated to them.

There's also a difference between delegation and abdication. Delegation requires clear goals, everyone has to know their responsibilities, and you need a checkup time. But you're basically letting the other person determine what to do, how, and when, reporting back to you periodically. When we abdicate, we tell someone to do something without being clear on what good behavior looks like or defining what we expect.

In delegation, we can intervene if necessary; in abdication, we say, "You take it," and then disappear, returning only to hit the other person when he makes a mistake. We call that "seagull management." Seagull managers fly in, make a lot of noise, dump on everybody, and fly out.

What about people who have few or no people reporting to them? Are these principles irrelevant?

No, they can pick up monkeys from peers, or at home, or from their kids. It doesn't matter if you have a managerial position; it matters that when somebody comes to you with an issue or problem, whether they work for you, are your boss, or a peer, that you talk with them and find out what's happening. But then you want to encourage them to make the next move, if possible.

Basically, we're talking about discretionary time. Would you say that should be a primary objective in effective time management?

Yes. You can spend all weekend getting organized, but if your boss calls you on Monday morning and says, "Boy, do I have an assignment for you!" and you have to do something different from what you planned, you don't have any discretionary time.

Our book deals basically with managing your people, but if you manage your boss well, you can anticipate what moves he might have in mind so there is less disruption to your schedule.

In recent years, you have committed your life to Jesus Christ. How did that come about?

I was named after a Presbyterian minister and attended Sunday School for eighteen years. In college I got away from attending church regularly, and spent much of my adult life out of the church. In 1982 and 1983, I started looking at the spiritual part of life again. *The One Minute Manager* was so absurdly successful, there was no way that I could take credit for it. I often wondered, "Who wrote that?" and concluded that God had to be behind it. Today, I consider myself a devout Christian with a better understanding of what being a Christian is all about. In a sense, it's like coming back home.

How have your Christian beliefs affected how you perceive the one minute manager?

The whole process has humbled me. I've become acutely aware that I don't own any of the concepts that I teach; they're all on loan. I've just been asked to shepherd some thoughts about working with people. I'm very excited about that ministry and feel I can make a difference if I just quiet myself and listen for God's guidance.

These concepts have been well-received because they work. Do you think there should be a deeper rationale for a Christian who strives to become a one minute manager?

Yes, because it's so consistent with Jesus' teachings. People talk about "management by wandering around." Jesus invented that.

He was very clear on goals, right from the beginning. He went from town to town, and if He caught people doing things right, He would praise them. If He thought people were out of whack, He would redirect them, and sometimes reprimand them.

As I read the Scriptures, I see situational leadership (based on individual skills and development) and the one-minute-manager approach as His philosophy of management. He hired twelve inexperienced people and built them into quite a group by setting goals, encouraging, redirecting, reprimanding. He did whatever was necessary to set up His plan. I've said for a long time, the most important thing about being a manager is not what happens when you're there, but what happens when you're not there. Jesus epitomizes servant leadership, which is working for your people and helping them win.

One Minute Manager-Isms'

Help people reach their full potential catch them doing something right.
— The One Minute Manager

As a manager the important thing is not what happens when you are there but what happens when you are not there.
— Putting the One Minute Manager to Work

There is nothing so unequal as the equal treatment of unequals.
— Leadership and the One Minute Manager

Anything worth doing does not have to be done perfectly—at first.
— Putting the One Minute Manager to Work

Things not worth doing are not worth doing well.
— The One Minute Manager Meets the Monkey

Empowerment is all about *letting go* so that others can *get going.*
— The One Minute Manager Builds High Performing Teams

Be still before the Lord
and wait patiently for him.

—Psalm 37:7

Decision Making

It's more than a coin toss

*B*ig decisions. Little decisions. Some monumental, some just pesky and annoying. They range from what TV show to watch, to what kind of car to buy, to whether it's time to make a career change.

Wouldn't life be a lot simpler if we didn't have to make decisions? We might not mind the decision-making process so much if we could have some kind of assurance that each decision we made would turn out right. Unfortunately, we can't—and they often don't.

Is there no hope? Are we sentenced to a lifetime of decision-making torment, forced to play Russian roulette with our futures?

There is no magic formula, no sure-fire strategy for arriving at decisions that never disappoint or fail. Even the Bible, which talks frequently about guidance, does not offer a specific, 1-2-3 series of steps for guaranteed success in every decision-making adventure. There are foundational biblically based guidelines, however, that can serve us well in dealing with decisions of all sizes. This section addresses many of these principles.

Chapter 17

Finding Direction

Dealing with difficult choices in a no-win situation

Thomas G. Clark

What would you do if you were asked by your company to become senior vice president of a chain of retail stores that had not made a profit in nine years—with the mandate of making the stores profitable in less than a year? Not only that, but what if the new assignment would mean reporting to a man you felt had demonstrated a clear dislike for you?

That was a situation I faced some years ago when my parent company, Hartmarx, asked me to transfer to J. P. Allen. Making a profit wasn't just a worthwhile goal. I was told the company "must and would" end the fiscal year—just eleven months away—in the black. It was like being named manager of a perpetually struggling baseball team and told that the team *would* make it to the World Series, no excuses.

If you're like me, your first impulse would be to say an emphatic "No!" I had no career death wish and wasn't at all tempted by this "no-win" situation. I felt that either the president of the struggling chain would demonstrate his animosity by trying to discredit me, or the company would fail again to make a profit—or both.

Seeking Direction

I felt considerable pressure to accept the transfer. I didn't know what to do. Fortunately, I remembered that I could consult with the One who knows all things. Even though I felt agreeing to such a move was foolish, I began to pray and study the Bible, seeking God's direction. In particular, I examined the Books of Proverbs and Psalms, appreciating the great wisdom I have gained from reading them during my years as a Christian.

My answer was in Psalm 57. I was reminded that the Lord provides refuge and protection for those who follow Him: "I cry out to God Most High, to God, who fulfills his purpose for me. He sends from heaven and saves me, rebuking those who hotly pursue me; God sends his love and his faithfulness" (57:2–3).

God Was in Control

That, I understood, was God's response to my dilemma. He was telling me to move out with peace and confidence, that He was in complete control despite the overwhelmingly negative circumstances.

God indeed proved Himself faithful. The company did make a profit that year—and for the next six years. Later, I was named president of the company, which fulfilled another of my goals.

Today, our uncertain economy is forcing many people to confront difficult decisions they would rather not face. While I was heading up the real estate division of Kuppenheimer Clothiers, I was acutely aware of that. I saw the difference at a convention of real estate professionals. In 1989, 11,000 people attended; in 1990, there were only 3,500.

"Ideally positioned" was not how you would describe my job. Across the board, the men's clothing sales were in a major slump.

When the economy is weak, men generally stop buying for themselves first. When the economy starts to recover, men's clothing seems to be among the last to find out.

For that reason, my company stopped its free-standing store expansion program for three years. The net result was a 50 percent staff reduction in my department, as well as uncertainty about the future of the real estate division in general.

Like most people in management, such a situation created anxiety for me. If the expansion didn't continue for the next three years, would my position be needed?

Being a good businessman, I began to weigh my alternatives. When I learned about an opening for a senior financial executive within the company, I thought it might be a good time to seek a more secure position. After all, my background is in finance.

But before I began to pursue the vacancy, I determined to seek God's will in the matter. Recalling the many times He had intervened in my business career, as well as my personal life—without any help on my part—I concluded that if the other position was where the Lord wanted me, He was fully able to bring it about.

I decided not to apply until I could feel confident of God's will in that situation. Reading through Psalms, Proverbs, and other books in the Bible, the only answer I received was, "Wait and trust God." I was reminded that my security is not in any job, but in God alone.

When I learned a short time later that the position I had considered was filled, I wasn't disappointed. I firmly believe that God is the real owner of everything on earth—even my company—and I know He will guide me as He sees best. He not only *wants* what is best for me; He *knows* what is best.

Decision-Making Checkpoints

Over the years, I have drawn a number of helpful principles from the Bible for solving business problems.

The foremost principle that undergirds them all is the "Great Commandment" (Matt. 22:36–37), which states that we are to love God with all our heart, soul, and mind. With that as a foundation, we can proceed with the following steps:

1. Seek God's will. (Jas. 4:13–15)
2. Be diligent. (Prov. 22:29)
3. Be industrious. (Rom. 12:6-8, 11–12)
4. Be honest. (2 Cor. 8:20–22)
5. Put God first. (Matt. 6:33–34)
6. Keep heaven in mind. (Matt. 6:19–21)
7. Give God His portion. (Mal. 3:8–12)
8. Avoid anxiety. (Luke 12:22–31)
9. Remember the fool. (Luke 12:15–21)

I have found that as we use these principles as checkpoints in our decision making, we not only grow in our relationship with God, but we also become more effective representatives of Jesus Christ in the market-place, and have more opportunities to tell and teach others about Him.

Chapter 18

Career Moves

The shortest route isn't always a straight line

Chip Weiant

Some of the most difficult decisions we face in life concern our careers: Where should I work? What kind of work should I do? I confronted those questions repeatedly several years ago.

For four years I worked as general manager of a hospitality organization in the Lake Erie Islands, north of Sandusky, Ohio. In 1987, however, I became dissatisfied. Like many resort areas, our organization had built much of its business around a clientele with alcohol problems. As a young Christian beginning to address some important issues for the first time, I concluded that I could not continue participating in that kind of environment.

It is best never to leave one job until you have another one to go to, but after much prayer, I decided there was no alternative but to tender my resignation.

This meant selling the lovely house that my wife, Anne, and I had painstakingly restored, along with many other material things to meet our immediate cash needs.

We moved to Columbus, Ohio, where my in-laws lived. Columbus was known for its dense corporate community of hospitality organizations, and I was convinced God wanted us in that city, although I didn't know what He had in mind.

With no job and no home, we moved in temporarily with Anne's parents. I remained unemployed for the next six months, although I investigated every possible opportunity. At a loss as to what to do, I concentrated my attention on God, spending countless, grueling hours in prayer, determined to discover what His plan was for me.

In retrospect, I can see that that *was* His plan—rather than changing my circumstances, He wanted to change me, breaking me (as it says in Ps. 51:17) and beginning the sometimes painful process of molding me into the person He wanted me to become.

New Opportunity

In March of 1988, I was asked to become project director for a new parachurch ministry, created to develop information systems to connect mission agencies around the world. It was a visionary plan and at first I thought, *This is it! Now I can work for the Lord full time.*

Operating out of loaned office space, part of my job was to raise funding for this enterprise. Six months later, despite working sixty hours a week, we were running out of money. I saw no hope of a dramatic turnaround, so I decided to renew my job search. Even though I agreed with the objective of the organization, I also knew that my first responsibility was to provide for my family, as 1 Timothy 5:8 tells us.

I learned one valuable lesson during my time with the organization: I concluded that I felt more suited to working in a secular environment. As followers of Jesus Christ, we are called to be "the salt of the earth." During the period I was employed by a Christian organization, I had the feeling that I was floating in saline solution. I wanted to be where I personally could make a difference.

Stopgap Measure

My next step was to become district manager for seven retirement centers in Ohio and Michigan. Almost from the start, I knew that was merely a stopgap measure until I found a position that more closely related to my interests in the hospitality industry.

The opportunity I had been looking for came in July of 1989, when I was hired to become director of operations for the Schmidt's Sausage Haus restaurant chain, which was founded in 1886. In the process, I became the first non-family member invited to join the executive committee.

Since that time, I have thoroughly enjoyed working for a highly respected company, with an excellent group of people. As a business, our primary objective is to make a profit. But I also see my job as an ideal way of representing Jesus Christ in the marketplace, ultimately seeking to advance His kingdom.

For example, I was very much involved in drafting our company's mission statement. This statement reads, "To successfully practice traditional hospitality in a manner which maximizes the gifts of our staff in order to optimally serve our guests, so that all might profit and grow both personally and professionally."

This noble philosophy, which fits well within a context of providing excellent service and reaping a reasonable profit, is essentially a paraphrased version of 1 Peter 4:9–10: "Offer hospitality to one another without grumbling. Each one should use whatever gift he has received to serve others, faithfully administering God's grace in its various forms." It is such a privilege to infuse scriptural principles into the marketplace environment. Here at Schmidt's we have established a standard of operations that affects the lives of more than four hundred people every day.

I don't see my role at Schmidt's in any sense as a "pastor," nor do I seek to impose my beliefs on others. But I have learned that the principles God has given through the Bible work wonderfully in the secular world. The end product of Christian activities, of course, is to glorify God, while the end product of secular business activities is profit. Our mission statement, I believe, is a way of achieving both.

Looking back, I'm thankful for how God has directed my career. My decisions were not always clear-cut; in fact, it took a somewhat roundabout route to get to where I am now. But I'm convinced that each step was important to His plan, preparing me for what lay ahead.

All the Right Moves

Chip Weiant has found the following elements helpful in decision making and problem solving:

1. What can I contribute?

"I ask myself what gifts God has given me that can be used in addressing this situation."

2. Stay in God's Word

"It's important to lay a foundation of personal godliness, seeking to get to know God in a deeper way each day. As we read and study the Bible daily, we can more quickly draw out spiritual principles that relate to the decision that needs to be made."

3. Seek counsel from other believers

"They can often help in pointing out considerations that we may not have thought about, as well as offering a different point of view."

4. Pray

"Once we become aware of the various alternatives, we can present them to the Lord and ask for His wisdom in evaluating them and determining which option is best. (Of course, we should be in prayer through the entire process.)"

5. Get in motion

"After receiving a sense of where we believe God is leading us, we need to get moving. At the same time, we need to continue going back to the other areas when necessary. The Bible tells us that God clearly directs our steps and is a light to our paths. That applies to all areas of life, including career, family, and finances."

Chapter 19

The Flip Side of Good Decisions

What happens when good decisions turn out to be bad?

Jeff Kobunski

What do you do when you examine all the pros and cons, test the facts according to the Word of God, pray, seek the advice of trusted friends, and finally, make a decision—and it still turns out wrong?

That's what happened to me early in 1989. My auto leasing company had been thriving for nearly two years. Karen, my wife, also had been working, but she was expecting our first child. I wanted her to be able to stay home and care for the baby.

When an opportunity was offered to expand my business with a used car sales lot, I liked the idea. We could eliminate our dependence on Karen's income, and with enough personnel, I could devote more of my time to the discipling ministry that I was having with other businessmen.

Determined not to act hastily, however, I prayed and consulted with Christian friends. I also asked myself several questions. For instance, I asked, "Will this simplify my life or complicate it?" A second question was, "How will this facilitate what I feel God wants us to do with our lives?"

My responses to both questions, I felt, clearly favored acquiring the used car lot. This seemed to be the Lord's means for enabling me to devote more time to helping people get to know God in a deeper way. In retrospect, I can see that I didn't analyze the situation as closely as I should have. I believe my motives were right—but my reasoning was faulty.

Admitting Failure

Almost immediately after buying the business, my life became more complicated. I had to familiarize myself with a similar— but different—business. There were new employees to get to know, and an inventory of cars to maintain. Instead of having more time, I found that I had less. The real answers to the questions I had asked, it turned out, were different from what I had anticipated.

Fortunately, the leasing business continued to do well, because used car sales fell far below expectations. At the end of a year—after losing $45,000—I had to face the painful decision of closing the newly acquired business.

I don't like to admit failure, so I struggled with what to do, but in the process God taught me some valuable lessons. For one thing, I realized my focus had been on what I could do for the Lord, in terms of giving of myself and my resources. He needed to show me that He was fully capable of carrying out His full agenda without my help.

My business difficulties also helped Karen and me come to grips with another poor decision we had made earlier. In 1986 we bought a large farm house on thirteen acres of land. Our intent was to use it for hospitality, to entertain guests and establish a ministry in the lives of couples we knew.

There was only one flaw in this scenario: I never consulted God about that decision. At the time, we felt we could afford the mortgage payments. We liked the house and proceeded to buy it. Not long afterward, we borrowed money to remodel much of the house. We never stopped to consider the long-term implications.

Since then, the house has been a continual financial drain. It's much more than what we need, and since we have spent so much time remodeling, our couples' ministry has never come about to the extent we envisioned.

When I decided to close the used car business, we also put our house up for sale. It was not an easy choice, considering the money and time invested, but we knew it was what God wanted us to do.

Eight months later, we still had not sold the house. In fact, it remained on the market for more than two years. With each passing day, we learned in a deeper way that God is in charge—a fact I should have considered before we bought the house. We were thankful for His promise in Jeremiah 29:11, "For I know the plans I have for you, declares the Lord, plans to prosper you and not to harm you, plans to give you hope and a future."

I'm learning to stick close to the Lord and never to presume to know His will. Poor decision making has consequences, and the Lord is not always obligated to bail us out immediately.

More Sensitive to Counsel

Sensitive to the dangers of self-reliance, I've learned to seek counsel more diligently from other Christians who might offer valuable insight. As it says in Proverbs 15:22, "Plans fail for lack of counsel, but with many advisers they succeed."

Karen and I also have studied biblical financial principles, discovering the virtues of a simpler lifestyle. God is calling men and women, I believe, to make tough decisions that run contrary to our complicated, materialistic society. For the past couple of years, He has been driving home to me the merits of a life free of the entanglements of debt and other unnecessary obligations.

It has taken us a long time to "simplify" our lives as much as we would like. Selling our house will be an important step. My wife and I have come to understand that for Christians to have a real impact on people, we have to be radically different. This includes our lifestyle, demonstrating we are not reliant on the material world for happiness and fulfillment.

In the future, I hope the radical difference in my life is also reflected more consistently by my decision making!

*There are different kinds of working,
but the same God works all of them
in all men.*

—1 Corinthians 12:6

Go, Team!

Reshaping America through teamwork

*F*or many years, "team" was a term relegated primarily to the playing fields, gymnasiums, and arenas of the world. In today's business environment, however, where everyone is clawing for a competitive advantage, team building is regarded as a key to success in the 1990s and beyond. The principle that two are better than one is eagerly being applied in small towns and megacities across America.

The principles of teamwork and team building, however, are hardly new. They are as old as the Bible and its central characters. In fact, the concept of two people being better than one comes directly from the Scriptures:

Two are better than one, because they have a good return for their work: If one falls down, his friend can help him up. But pity the man who falls and has no one to help him up! Also, if two lie down together, they will keep warm. But how can one

keep warm alone? Though one may be overpowered, two can defend themselves. A cord of three strands is not quickly broken.
— Ecclesiastes 4:9–12

It seems ironic then that even within the Christian community, teamwork has not been widely practiced. The "lone ranger" or independent operator approach to ministry and personal piety has been much more enthusiastically embraced. Slowly, however, the team concept is gaining favor as more people and organizations test and confirm its validity.

This section is devoted to examining the idea of team building from several perspectives, suggesting some practical how-tos as well as presenting some supportive case studies. We trust that by the time you finish reading, you too will burst forth with a hearty and enthusiastic, "Go, Team!"

Chapter 20

Common Goals

Pulling together is crucial for success

Dave Stoddard

TEAMWORK: Cooperative effort by the members of a group or team to achieve a common goal.

All across America, companies are increasingly recognizing the value of teamwork—or more accurately, team building. The number one advantage they are realizing is greater productivity, the practical result of the ancient principle that two are better than one. Taking a group and building it into a team fosters synergy, creativity, and a sense of innovation that individuals could not achieve on their own. Corporate America is seeing how team building helps to broaden vision and sharpen the focus, enabling companies to maintain the competitive edge that is so essential in today's ever-changing world.

During my ten years as a sales representative for Kendall Health Care, a medical supplies and health care equipment manufacturer based in Atlanta, Georgia, I saw many examples of the benefits of team building in working with customers and other employees. Over those years I was consistently one of the company's top producers, yet it took me considerably less time to get the same results as other sales reps. It wasn't because I had greater sales ability, but simply because I let my customers know—and feel—that they were part of my team.

Customer Comes First

In my mind, the customer always came first. If a customer had a complaint about our service or one of our products, the customer had every right to see that complaint rectified. My role, as I saw it, was that of a servant—serving the customer as well as the people within my company.

By maintaining open and honest communication, my customers always felt a sense of ownership of what I was doing for them. The interesting thing is, once people have ownership in an endeavor, they begin to take a more active role and actually do a lot of the work for you.

I didn't do this to manipulate or take advantage of people. It was merely a practical application of a biblical teaching. Philippians 2:3–4 says, "Do nothing out of selfish ambition or vain conceit, but in humility consider others better than yourselves. Each of you should look not only to your own interests, but also to the interests of others." When people saw that I was sincerely concerned about their needs, they were more than willing to work with me.

This did not happen immediately, however. When I first took over my sales territory, Kendall had zero credibility. In fact, most of my customers did not like my company at all. I remember one of them telling me, "You don't need to come back. We won't be doing business with you."

Ready to Serve

Rather than make a hasty retreat, I responded, "I really respect how you feel. What happened?" After the customer explained the problems he had encountered, I emphasized that I was there to serve him and considered it a privilege to be of assistance in any way possible. Of course, many customers took a wait-and-see attitude, but when I began demonstrating that I meant what I said, almost without exception they turned around and gave me significant business.

I worked primarily with hospitals and regarded the products and equipment I sold as ways of helping the hospital staffs provide greater medical care for their patients. Dealing with the hospital bureaucracy can be incredibly complicated and time-consuming, so instead I concentrated on making strategic contacts. These were people who could understand the value of the products I was selling and knew the best ways for speeding up the decision-making process.

Working with Experts

Most of the time I would ask for their suggestions on how to get my products into the hospital. I would make them a part of my team, telling them, "You're the expert. You know this hospital better than I do. I'm just here to serve you, and I'd really appreciate your help and counsel on how we can best get this product considered." Often, they would set up appointments for me with key people. These individuals were already receptive because of the credibility I had established with my initial contacts.

Again, this required perseverance. I remember one time it took four months for me to get a meeting with a physician so I could tell him about new anticlotting equipment we had developed for use in operating rooms. But when I finally got to see him and began building a working relationship with him, he not only helped in getting the equipment into the hospital in record time, but also conducted meetings with other physicians so they could learn about the benefits of the equipment.

Because of this physician's help and support, the hospital became one of my largest users of this particular piece of equipment.

Importance of Attitude

I have discovered that a key to team building is the attitude of the leader. He must be willing to give up control, letting the people working with him become an integral part of what he is trying to accomplish. Basically, it amounts to creating an environment in which people can flourish by using their gifts and talents. When the customer has ownership and becomes "boss," barriers in the relationship come down.

This is what happened with the network of customers I worked with in my sales territory. The more experience I gained and the more confidence they had in me, the less work I actually had to put into the sales process.

Who's to Blame?

I think of one irate customer who ordered a large amount of anesthesia products. The dealer failed to deliver the supplies when promised, and although I had been assured of prompt delivery, the hospital had not received the product. Surgeries are an important part of what hospitals do, and if there is no anesthesia, you can't do surgery. So you can imagine how high the tension level was.

My customer called, demanding immediate action. "You're the one who's fully responsible," he said. "I don't want to hear about your dealer's problems. You dropped the ball!"

Even though I had been assured by the dealer that the problem had been corrected—which it obviously was not—I agreed. "You're right, I take full responsibility. What do you want me to do?" After he reprimanded me, I told the customer how much I appreciated his feedback and assured him that I would not only work to see that the supplies were quickly received, but also that this incident would make me a better sales rep.

Within a month this same tough customer gave me an order worth $100,000 that I had not done anything to get. My dealer and company were dumbfounded. "How did you do it?" they asked.

Working for Mutual Benefit

It was simply a matter of integrity, humility, and the customer's understanding that we were a team, working together for our mutual good.

Traditionally, business has focused on efficiency, but I have found in dealing with people that the key is effectiveness. You can be efficient in working with things, but with people you need to be effective. This is best approached from a biblical perspective: doing for others as you would have them do for you; putting their interests first; and most of all, seeking to honor God in everything you do.

Within a Christian context, this sense of team is referred to as "community." As we read in Romans 12, we are part of one vast spiritual body, but we each have been given different gifts and abilities to contribute to the whole. When used properly, this fosters a healthy interdependence where everyone can play an important part and achieve extraordinary results.

As businessmen, we are vitally interested in what works. Team building, based on the truth in Ecclesiastes 4:9—"Two are better than one, because they have a good return for their work"—is something that works.

Chapter 21

Rallying a City: An Olympian Effort

Atlanta focuses inward as well as outward

Dale Jones

The 1994 Super Bowl and the Summer Olympics in 1996 are evidence of an incredible amount of time, energy, and finances that have been invested in Atlanta over the past few years. Although much of that effort is being directed toward the sporting events themselves, a significant amount will be focused toward even more important pursuits.

Around the world, sports have traditionally been great rallying points for people, and we wanted to capitalize on the positive momentum of the Super Bowl and the Olympics to mobilize our city's churches and ministries to work together in a Christ-centered way.

Enter Quest Atlanta '96. This coordinating council was established to strengthen Atlanta's commitment to meet the spiritual and human needs of the local community, as well as the thousands of visitors who will be coming to the city over the next several years.

Unity Is the Goal

When I became Quest's executive director in July 1991, I set out to help in achieving this goal—as Jesus prayed in John 17:21–23—"that all of them may be one. . . . brought to complete unity." But in this quest to bring together Atlanta's diverse community, 1994 and 1996 serve only as benchmarks. The cornerstone of our endeavor is to encourage a unity among the body of Christ in Atlanta that will live long beyond the events.

In principle, this sounds like a great idea. But how does this become a reality? We envision new bridges being built, partnerships being forged that otherwise might never come about. This would require a very special form of teamwork.

While we have not yet "arrived" at our goal, several keys steps have been taken that have brought about remarkable progress. The first was the vision of Mrs. Deen Day Smith, former Georgia Governor Joe Frank Harris, and former Atlanta Mayor Andrew Young, and later, businessman Truett Cathy, who stepped forward to endorse a united effort to improve our community. Their influence was essential to starting the Quest Atlanta '96 coalition.

Building on Diversity

A second step was the selection of a board of directors of men and women to represent our city's cultural and spiritual diversity. Mrs. Ida Bell was appointed to chair the ten-member board.

Then we began involving the entire Atlanta community of 2.5 million people and eighteen hundred churches of all sizes. Over six hundred pastors and church leaders were brought together to share their vision for the city. As a result, six focus areas were identified:

▲ Housing and community development

▲ International partnerships and hospitality

▲ Youth sports

▲ Christ-centered outreaches

▲ Prayer

▲ Denominational leaders

Three additional focus groups or committees—business and civic leaders, ministries, and churches—were established later. Our intent was to link similar ministries and organizations, helping them to work together toward a common goal.

A noble purpose and broad representation, however, guarantee neither teamwork nor unity. Differences of doctrine, philosophy, mission, or methodology could easily foster division rather than harmony. For this reason, from the start we placed great emphasis on prayer. For something of this magnitude to succeed, we knew God would have to play a prominent role.

Transcending Differences

We found that prayer served as a strong unifying factor, enabling us to transcend our differences and helping us to appreciate the great value of working in partnership through Jesus Christ. As the saying goes, the whole is greater than the sum of the parts.

All of us involved in Quest Atlanta '96 are keeping this concept in the forefront of our thinking. Everyone will benefit through this unique partnership, enabling us to become better and stronger in pursuing our individual missions.

To date, more than four hundred of our churches already have Quest representatives. At a recent retreat, twenty-five pastors from different denominations met to discuss how they could best team up together. And some urban and suburban churches are beginning to tear down old barriers by holding joint worship services and combining some ministry programs.

This is not to say that we have not encountered resistance. There have been some groups intent upon building their own plans that have not been willing to cooperate with others through Quest. For some ministries and churches, the idea of partnership and cooperation is foreign. They are accustomed to functioning autonomously.

Separate But Unified

Other churches or organizations fear that they will have to give up their identities to team up with other groups. But more and more, many of these groups are realizing they can remain who they are and still be in partnership with others.

As we continue to focus on our common vision and values, everybody is beginning to feel a sense of shared ownership, rather than a "me and my program" attitude.

The Olympics will be our one moment in time, so to speak, a once-in-a lifetime event when the world will literally be on our doorstep. (According to one estimate, there will be 15,000 athletes, another 15,000 journalists, and 450,000 people from more than 200 countries who will attend as spectators.) We all understand that we cannot allow differences to divide us. It will be an unparalleled opportunity for churches to work together in ministering to people who come to visit our city, as well as those who live here.

Chapter 22

T.E.A.M. (together everyone achieves more)

Survival lessons for the battlefield and business

David R. Willcox

One of the best lessons I ever learned in team building came in 1951, while I was at Fort Benning, Georgia, in Infantry Officers Candidate School. Out of the 286 original candidates that enrolled, there were only 86 of us who graduated twenty-one weeks later as second lieutenants. That in itself built a significant amount of esprit de corps, but it was an experience during the eighteenth week that profoundly influenced my appreciation of team interaction.

During the preceding weeks, we had drilled and drilled. Part of the process was swapping roles with each other, from the company commander to rifleman to radio man to squad leader. Frankly, we had regarded this as tedious and unnecessary.

However, we did learn each other's jobs well. We watched each other and learned from our mistakes, we critiqued each other, solved problems together, and our goals were clear, understood, and agreed upon. As a result, we grew to trust one another.

In the eighteenth week we were on a night exercise and I lost contact with the man on my left. Momentarily the thought passed through my mind that our advancing line had been broken, but just as quickly I relaxed. Because we had exchanged roles in training, I knew exactly what the next man to my left would do and knew what I must do to regain the integrity of our line. Best of all, I knew that he knew that I knew.

I felt like a cartoon character with a light bulb flashing over his head. Suddenly I knew what the training was all about. We had become a team by working together, living together, and understanding each other's roles.

Principle into Practice

One year later, I was able to put this principle into live action. It was in the Chor Wan valley of Korea. I had been given command of a rifle platoon that had been decimated by casualties. These were twenty-two tired, demoralized, and frightened individuals. There should have been forty-four men. I decided to try passing on what I learned in Officers Candidate School.

We built back up to forty-four soldiers, and every third week we went back in reserve, but instead of letting them sleep, drink, and play cards, we ran platoon exercises up and down hills. We swapped jobs, got to know each other and our individual capacities. I didn't win any popularity contests; even my fellow officers thought I was too "gung ho."

But on July 7–10, 1953, this training paid off. We and two other platoons were on Pork Chop Hill and were surrounded for three days by eight divisions of Chinese—thousands of enemy soldiers. The other platoons were pushed off the hill, but my guys held their positions.

In the first few hours of the battle, I was wounded and cut off from the rest of my command. Our hand-held radio did not work, so communications were nonexistent. But through our drills, we had become a fighting team that could function even without me.

We trusted each other, knowing that we would look out for one another. A number of our men sustained wounds in the fighting, but not a single life was lost. When the fighting ended, we all got off the hill together.

Keys to Survival

The keys to survival were simple. Today, nearly forty years later, they apply to any setting, especially business:

1. Purpose. We knew why we were there.

2. Roles. We knew what each other's jobs were and how they related to ours.

3. Goals. We understood the specifics that were required to carry out our purpose.

4. Trust. We could work together because we had built up trust and confidence in one another.

In 1 Corinthians 12:12–26, we see that these concepts come directly from the Bible. This passage talks about the body (the human body as well as the body of Christ) being a single unit, made up of many parts. These parts, with different functions, operate in harmony for a common purpose, supporting one another.

As it says in 1 Corinthians 12:25, "there should be no division in the body, but . . . its parts should have equal concern for each other." This, I believe, is an essential element for effective team building, whether it be on a playing field, in a corporate office, or in a church building: parts working together, carrying out different roles but striving for a common objective.

Chapter 23

The Sense God Gave a Goose

Honk if you love teamwork

James S. Hewett

The next time you see geese flying in V formation, you might be interested in knowing why they fly that way.

As each bird flaps its wings, it creates an uplift for the bird immediately following. By flying in a V formation, the whole flock adds at least 71 percent greater flying range than if each bird flew on its own. (Christians who share a common direction and a sense of community can reach their objective quicker and easier, because they are traveling on the thrust of one another.)

Whenever a goose falls out of formation, it suddenly feels the drag and resistance of trying to go it alone, and quickly gets back into formation to take advantage of the lifting power of the bird immediately in front. (If we had as much sense as a goose, we would stay in formation with those who are headed the same way we are going.)

When the lead goose gets tired, he rotates back in the wing and another goose flies point. (It pays to take turns doing hard jobs—with people at church or with geese flying south.) The geese honk from behind to encourage those up front to keep up their speed. (What do *we* say when we honk from behind?)

Finally, when a goose gets sick, or is wounded by a shot and falls out, two geese fall out of formation and follow him down to help and protect him. They stay with him until he is either able to fly, or until he is dead, and then they launch out on their own or with another formation to catch up with their original group. (If people knew we would stand by them like that in church, they would push down the walls to get in.)

From Illustrations Unlimited, *Edited by James S. Hewett* © *1988, used by permission of Tyndale House Publishers, all rights reserved.*

*I press on toward the goal to win the prize
for which God has called me.*

—Philippians 3:14

Goal Setting: Critical to Success

*W*hat specific plans have you established at work, with your family, or for personal growth in specific areas? How clearly have you defined goals you intend to pursue today, next week, this month, or throughout the year?

We would all agree that planning and goal setting are valuable to our pursuit of success in any area of life. But how many of us are confident that our plans and goals are well-conceived, carefully stated, and carried out with vigor? Several business authorities would sum up the situation this way: "People don't plan to fail—they fail to plan." Does this describe you, or someone you know?

Too often, our plans and goals are established by default. Because we do not take the time to define them, other people are more than happy to do so. We carry out *their* plans and aim at *their* goals, all the while repressing the gnawing feeling that we would rather be doing—or be striving toward—something else.

General Douglas MacArthur once said, "In war, when a commander becomes so bereft of reason and perspective that he fails to understand the dependence of arms on Divine guidance, he no longer understands victory." For the Christian in business, understanding that God is central to the long-term success of any endeavor makes a great difference in what goals and objectives we set—and how we carry them out.

Proverbs 19:21 tells us, "Many are the plans in a man's heart, but it is the Lord's purpose that prevails." God maintains a vital interest in the outcome of all our plans, regardless of how insignificant they may seem. As we go through the planning and goal setting process, He is the one who helps to answer the question, "Why?" He provides the underlying rationale, our motivation, for doing what we do.

Chapter 24

Driven by Vision, Mission, and Values

Why are we in business anyway?

Randal Walti

"Why are you in business?" Every time I ask chief executive officers that question, nine out of ten will say, "To make money, of course!" That's their first reaction, but usually when they dig deeper a different reason surfaces. There was some driving force, a purpose, that motivated them to start the business in the first place.

The first part of any planning process must start with a clear statement of purpose. Some of us call this a "company charter." We try to narrow it down to concise answers to three questions: Why are you in business? What business are you in? and, What values do you hold dear and inviolate in the process of doing business?

Many of my clients have asked to skip this part of the process so they can get to the "nuts and bolts" of their business. But I tell them that to be effective, they must get their teams aligned with a common purpose.

The Power of Alignment

Power comes from a clear sense of purpose. Proverbs 29:18 says, "Where there is no vision, the people perish" (KJV). When a team of horses pulls in the same direction, they can do much more work than they could if each pulled individually. But what would happen if they were teamed to pull in opposite directions? Obviously, they would go nowhere.

Business leaders have discovered that the days are over when workmates can be *commanded* to go in the same direction. Instead, they first must be *convinced* of the value of the company's purpose. Why is it important and in their best interests to be aligned? If they aren't convinced, they may give lip service, but will not buy into the purpose. Their performance will prove it.

Think about the last time you became really excited about something. Chances are, you first had to be convinced of its significance before you felt any enthusiasm for it. The people who work for you (or with you) are no different.

Where Do You Start?

In defining your purpose, your focus should be clear and concise. If your purpose is too complicated to remember, what good is it?

When we meet with CEOs, we often ask them to rank the following statements in order of importance, in relation to each other. The vision statement should embody the original dream of the founder, usually a combination of two or more of the following:

▲ To do significant work.

▲ To build a successful organization.

▲ To build a strong financial foundation.

▲ To serve our customers.

▲ To inspire others.

▲ To be challenged.

▲ To have fun and enjoy our work.

▲ To provide an empowering environment.

▲ To grow as individuals.

▲ To exploit exciting new ideas.

One example of a vision statement is:

To be an inspirational force in the growth
and prosperity of our clients.

Keep it short and to the point. Share it with clients, employees, and suppliers. Make it the focus of everything the company does or tries to accomplish.

What's My Line?

The next step is a mission statement that should answer the question, "What is your business?" What are the specifics of the products or services you provide? The mission statement generally embodies three or four elements, including a strategic view, a tactical view, and a relational view.

This probably is the easiest part of the company charter, because it is what we answer when asked, "What's your line?" An example is:

We coach CEOs in the development of prosperous enterprise founded on their long-term values. We assist clients in developing and implementing innovative marketing, financial, information technology, and organization development programs that yield meaningful results. We invest our talents to build lasting relationships with our clients.

How Do We Do It?

What values do we hold dear? This part of the company charter helps identify the most important means for accomplishing the vision. For Christians in the business world, this is perhaps the most challenging aspect of the charter. This is where we often must engage in the conflict between what the world tells us is acceptable and what God says is right.

While articulating our values is challenging, it is also dangerous. They essentially give our associates permission to hold us accountable. If we don't uphold our values, we are open targets for criticism, even ridicule. But what an opportunity to establish a strong value system to guide corporate operations, and then be able to explain the basis of our values is our relationship to God.

Which values should be expressed? The following list is a good place to start. Select five or six that are most important to you; then state them in a way that is meaningful for your business.

▲ Honesty and integrity

▲ Commitment to our customers

▲ Growth and dignity of our employees

▲ Income tied to service

▲ High self-discipline

▲ Offering the latest in technology

▲ Empowering corporate environments to foster our outstanding results

▲ Continuous learning

▲ Clarity in communications

▲ Truth in understanding

▲ Responsibility

▲ Quality of products (or service) as our highest priority

▲ Excellence in everything we do

Once the CEO has gone through these steps and arrived at a rough draft he likes, it is important to allow the key managers to tear it apart and rebuild it from the ground up. Remember the team of horses at the beginning of the article: If they are pulling in opposing directions, there will be no progress.

As painful as it may be, these statements of vision, mission, and values must be adopted equally by everyone involved if the company is to benefit from their combined strength pulling in the same direction. If your personnel can't buy into your company charter, making it their own, your business enterprise will encounter continual frustration and futility.

With a commonly held, clearly defined, and understood company charter, however, the business may exceed your expectations. The steps of planning and goal setting may be comparatively simple exercises. Once you know where you are going, *then* you can determine how to get there and how to know when you have arrived.

Chapter 25

A Golden Thumb Planning Strategy

Make personal goals work for you

Millard N. MacAdam

A new worker mentality is revolutionizing business environments all around the planet. Today, many men and women want to work to live, not live to work. They want to be involved with their employers in setting goals, have a piece of the business action and, at the same time, find meaning and fulfillment in their jobs.

Satisfaction is the operative word to the workers of today. They want a sense that, through their work, they are contributing to a purpose greater than themselves. They want dignity. They desire meaningful relationships with fellow workers and managers.

Most people, however, fail to find these qualities on a sustained basis. The problem is not their jobs, but the lack of a biblical view of their purpose in life—and the purpose of work. People who establish a balanced set of goals for all aspects of their lives—goals derived through well-defined spiritual values—generally find joy and meaning through goals they achieve in the workplace.

In the Bible, God establishes clear principles about work:

▲ You cannot serve two masters. God will supply all your needs. (Matt. 6:24–34)

▲ Keep eternity foremost in your mind when doing work, and enjoy all your labor during the few years God has given you. (Eccl. 3:12–15; 5:18)

▲ If you don't work, you don't eat. (2 Thess. 3:10)

▲ Cultivate and keep things in good shape. (Gen. 2:15; 3:17–19)

▲ Understand that the fruits of your labor may be unsatisfying in the long run, often painful and grievous; your mind may not always rest at night; and labor itself is good. (Eccl. 2:18–24)

When people develop goals at work in light of biblical principles like these, they usually experience less stress. This, in turn, helps them to achieve personal and job-related goals more easily.

We Plan, God Guides

God wants us to plan our course by having a vision and mission *(see Randall Walti's chapter)*, targeting key goals, and outlining measurable objectives and tasks necessary for accomplishing those goals (Prov. 16:9). But at the same time, He wants us to acknowledge that He is the one who guides our steps to achieve them. We may have many plans and intentions, but the Lord's purpose will prevail (Prov. 19:21).

Some people aggressively avoid planning and goal setting. They tend to take better care of their cars than they do of their lives and businesses. But like a well-running car, lives and businesses that run well can provide excitement, pleasure, and satisfaction. They also require regular diagnosis and service, sometimes repairs.

"Gold Thumb" Performers

As a business consultant, I facilitate a diagnostic process to help corporate leaders find "toxic" elements in their operations that impede productivity and restrict cash flow. In the process, I find people who maintain a broad, balanced set of goals for all aspects of their lives. These "nontoxic" individuals stand out like "golden thumbs" as top performers and producers, contributing to the organization's overall health, not to its harm. Often these people share the following characteristics:

1. They understand their life purpose from God's point of view and have conceptualized and written down their vision, driving values, mission, goals, and objectives. (They haven't just thought about them.)

2. They have discussed these items with others, asking for feedback and suggestions for improvement.

3. They use a variety of strategies to review goals and reinforce them on a regular basis. This can include recording them in a calendar book, on a computer, in the front of their Bible, in a notebook, or on an audiotape to play periodically while traveling to and from work.

How do they arrive at these values, goals, and strategies? On the next page is a "goal wheel" that represents each major area of a person's life. This chart helps people see the importance of maintaining a relative balance between the goals they set for these specific areas.

You will notice that the spiritual "spoke" of the goal wheel penetrates the "hub." This is because the spiritual dimension of a person's life is central to how he pursues the other areas. This spoke provides strength, unity, and stability, serving as the starting point for goal setting. The spiritual goals, therefore, become a foundational part of all other goals.

I have never known a person who achieved perfect balance in his or her life and, except for Jesus Christ, I don't think it is possible. It is possible and practical, however, to fill in each of the "spokes" of our lives with thoughtfully selected, spiritually driven goals. Try establishing your spiritual growth goals first, then use those as a springboard for goals in the other aspects of your life—including work. I believe you will find your work has more meaning, enabling you to work harder and with greater joy than those who ignore the spiritual dimension of life.

Goal Wheel Chart

Think of each area of your life as a part of your goal wheel with your spiritual part as the key to align the hub of your wheel to support the other areas of your life. Chart the total from each of the ten groups on the wheel. Color in each part to gain a perspective on the relative balance you presently have in your life. Are you pleased with what you see? Is your goal wheel running smoothly? If not, what new goals could help you achieve the balance you want in your life? Use your insights to set new goals and develop different areas in your life. In achieving the

proper balance and becoming a more well-rounded individual, each of the other areas of your life will become more fulfilling and satisfying, and will enhance your personal effectiveness.*

Striking Gold with Top Performers

"Golden thumb" performers are an asset to any organization because of their high levels of performance and productivity. Everyone wants them, but I'm often asked, "Where do they come from?"

Most often, I find them in companies headed by Christian business leaders who have diligently developed the key elements of what I call a "goal-achieving organizational culture" that supports people of high character, competence, and commitment. These enterprises commonly enjoy good cash flow, low turnover and absenteeism, high morale, and focus on the development of a Total Integrity Management System[SM] built on a formula that includes accountability to the company's driving values, total quality, and continuous, measurable improvement.

Here are some tips on how to create a motivating, goal-achieving organizational culture through Total Integrity Management. [SM]

▲ Encourage people to live balanced, value-driven lives based on a solid moral standard. This will guide their decisions, as well as help align their walk with their talk. A moral standard is the only way to avoid the modern-day trap of "situational ethics" that encourages lying, cheating, and stealing.

▲ Develop shared values. These are the driving forces for achieving your organization's vision, mission, and goals. At every level of the organization, people need to know, support, and hold each other accountable for living out these corporate values.

▲ Have people share results and goals they set with one another in working groups or teams. Support each other by celebrating successes and providing coaching, counsel, and feedback on results not achieved.

▲ Conduct values audits. These audits are valuable in revealing discrepancies between *professed* (spoken or written) values and *expressed* values (reflected in actual behavior). This helps people "walk" and "talk" values in a more congruent way, building trust and adding positive energy to the workplace.

▲ Honor people of character, competence, and commitment. Individuals who personify the values of your organization deserve special recognition.

▲ Develop celebrations and ceremonies. Such events bond people together and to the organization. They should be fun and crazy, not overly serious or formal.

▲ Tell corporate stories. Success stories of people with character, competence, and commitment, who have lived out the corporate values in the face of adversity or personal risk, should become sagas to communicate your corporate culture to employees new and old.

▲ Maintain a diverse network of honest players. These people carry the culture and preside over it. Encourage them to express their personal differences and preferences to keep business alive and open, on track, creative, and of high integrity.

A commitment to each of these steps, I am convinced, will help to develop balanced, spiritually centered goal-setting skills for yourself and among your staff. The product will be people of character, competence, and commitment, a healthy organization, and high levels of future achievement for your company.

*Adapted from "Beyond Business As Usual: Strategies for Balancing Ethics and the Enterprise." Copyrighted 1991, Millard N. MacAdam.

Chapter 26

Four Steps for Achieving Goals

How to finish what you start

Hugh B. Jacks

In business, we often hear about the merits of setting goals. Unfortunately, not everyone understands how to formulate worthwhile goals and carry them to completion. During the course of my career, it has been my observation that an effective goals program has four parts.

Put it in writing. Number one, the goal needs to be stated in terms of what will be present when it is reached, and must be in writing.

For instance, if you simply say you have a goal to lose some weight, you do not have a good goal because it is neither specific nor measurable. But if you say that you want to go from 175 pounds to 165 pounds, and from a 35-inch waist to a 34-inch waist, by a certain date, you will have lived up to the definition of a good goal. You have explained exactly what will be present when the goal is reached, and there is no rationalization. You either do it or you don't do it; you're either moving toward it or you're not.

Make it a priority. Once the goal has been written and can be seen clearly, we come to the matter of priorities. Ask and answer the question, "How important is this goal?" Is it a wish, a want, a desire, or is it really a priority in your life? One writer says that as businessmen, we spend approximately 80 percent of our time doing the wrong things because we don't have the right priorities. He's correct, but this also applies to other professions, our churches, even our homes.

The problem is: *Goals never equal outcome. Priorities always do.* One man approached me after a speech and told me that as a young man, he had dreamed of having a close-knit, happy family. Finally he got that family, but instead of going to his family, his priorities went to his personal finances, his job, and his hobbies. The result was that he lost his family to divorce. He had a goal to have a happy family, but it never became a priority for him.

Schedule it. Once we know what we want and feel certain it's a priority in our life, it becomes a matter of how to get it into action. The schedule is the only way—an annual, monthly, weekly, daily, hourly schedule—that we can turn dreams into reality, because that propels our action.

Every time I say that, I see someone in the audience frowning. I interpret that to mean, "Not me. I'm not going to have a ball and chain of a schedule," but the fact is—everyone has a schedule. The question is not whether you have a schedule, but rather, according to whose schedule are you working? Whose goals are you pursuing? Whose priorities are you living? Are they yours, and are they well thought out?

Follow through. Once the schedule is decided, it's a matter of discipline. By this I mean maintaining commitment to our goals and priorities during times of pressure. There are always stresses on the job, in the home, and in our communities that can pull us away from our well-intended goals and priorities. Only through discipline—determining that our goals and priorities are worth keeping and striving to attain, no matter what—can we successfully follow through on them.

One more thing: Make certain God is a key part of the process. Over the years, I learned these principles from a variety of motivational books and tapes. I got the process down pat and found that it worked. One day, however, it occurred to me that while I had learned how to be successful, I never really learned how I could *enjoy* success, or how to really be secure.

I would get a promotion, a raise, or some recognition and be very excited for a few days. But before I knew it, I would be right back to seeking security all over again. I started to wonder about all the books I had read, thinking perhaps they had left off a chapter.

Then someone told me that insecurity is simply building one's life around someone or something that can be taken away. It was only after committing my life to Jesus Christ that I found real security.

I still keep setting goals just as ardently as I ever have; I just set them from a different perspective now. As I read the Bible, looking strictly for what it says about business principles, I found that I could throw away every other book about becoming successful in business (and I have hundreds of them) and still be successful just by applying the principles in the Scriptures.

Proverbs 16:3 says, "Commit to the Lord whatever you do, and your plans will succeed." My work life hasn't changed that much since 1969, when Christ became my Savior and Lord. The one difference is, God has established my plans. As I grasped this principle, my goals have fallen into place. Today, I have three primary goals in life:

▲ To give God rightful ownership of my life.

▲ To be a living interpretation of God's Word to the greatest degree possible to those around me.

▲ To help others to know and to grow in Christ, just as others have helped me to know and grow in Him.

Under each, I list details on how it is to be achieved. Can you think of any more worthwhile goals, both for the short term and the long term?

Chapter 27

More than Just Fun and Games

A family vacation that made a difference

William Terry, M.D.

The family vacation: a great American tradition. Find a fun location with lots of fun activities and get away from it all. Rest, relax, and recharge. Doesn't that sound great?

It sounds good to me, too, and over the years I have enjoyed a few of these. But as a fifty-nine-year-old workaholic physician (now retired), I and my wife, Eloise, felt a real need to begin incorporating more substance into our annual gathering with our children and grandchildren.

For Eloise and me, this became a prayerful and yet practical exercise in planning and goal setting. What kind of "substance" did we want to include, and how could we do it in a way that appealed to our children and their mates?

We agreed on the "what" almost immediately. First, in addition to modeling our Christian faith, it was our desire to communicate the biblical values concerning marriage and family life that have come to mean so much to us.

Second, we also felt a need to impart to our children the biblical principles about personal financial management that we have learned and found useful over the years. For example, we cannot serve both God *and* money (Matt. 6:24), God owns it all (Job 41:11), we are to be faithful stewards of the Lord's resources (1 Cor. 4:2), the pitfalls of debt (Prov. 22:7; Rom. 13:8), the importance of giving (Prov. 3:9), and the practical importance of a budget and determining "how much is enough."

The question became, how do we go about doing this and have our fun, too?

Converging on Disney World

We all agreed to converge on Orlando, Florida, between Thanksgiving and Christmas 1991. Eloise and I would cash in some condominium time-shares we had accumulated and re-deem frequent flyer miles to provide some of the transportation.

Walt Disney World had already been selected as a focal point for our time together, but Eloise wrote to each of our children ahead of time to explain the ground rules. We told them that while most of the days would be spent taking in the Disney attractions, one day would be spent discussing money manage-ment from a biblical perspective. Then, on four evenings, Eloise would meet separately with the women and I similarly with the men, to talk about the foundations for building God-honoring marriages and families.

Although a few questions were asked, none of the children expressed opposition to our plans. We proceeded with the prepa-rations, praying that it would be a meaningful time for everyone. Our youngest son, David, and his wife, Dolly, would be unable to join us because of work commitments, so we arranged to videotape our sessions so they could participate indirectly.

Family Seminar on Finances

The financial planning day was coordinated with a consultant friend of ours, Scott Houser of Ronald Blue and Co., Atlanta.

Over the past couple of years, we had gotten to know and appreciate Scott's wisdom and he accepted our invitation to lead the family seminar.

He spoke for a couple of hours, then Eloise and I shared our testimony with emphasis on how biblical teaching has influenced and motivated some financial decisions we had made about our estate, in particular our desire to continue being involved in the financial support of God's work.

We wanted to help them gain a good grasp of these principles at a much earlier stage in their families than we did—passing on biblical wisdom before whatever inheritance they might receive. Then Scott had private time with each couple for personal consultation.

Personal Update

During the men's and women's sessions about marriage and family, Eloise and I updated the kids on what God had generally been doing in our lives personally and why we feel it is so important to continue sharing the love of Jesus Christ with them, with our grandchildren, and with others.

We drew from a number of resources, including the "Dad, the Family Shepherd" seminar; a convicting message called "The Three Chairs" by Bruce Wilkinson; a stirring testimony from Nancy Leigh DeMoss at the 1991 Christian Business Men's Committee Convention; and other insights we had learned over the years through our involvement in CBMC.

I explained to the guys about the importance of being godly men and spiritual leaders for their families. Eloise shared with the ladies from her own experience as a wife, a mother, and her years teaching Bible Study Fellowship, relating to the lordship of Jesus Christ in their lives.

As the weekend concluded, my wife and I felt we had achieved our goal. We had enjoyed the "fun and games," but felt the time together was much more than that. Judging from all the comments of our children, they felt the same way—it won the prize for our most memorable week together.

Even though our kids are grown and have their own families, Eloise and I realize the impact we still can have on them and the grandchildren. By God's grace, we want that impact to point them to Jesus.

We're thankful that God gave us this unique opportunity to relate as a family, and we're planning similar family gatherings for the future.

No Time for Retirement

Retirement, for many people, means bidding farewell to a fruitful career, easing back in life, and "getting a chance to do what I want to do." In that regard, William Terry is not your typical retiree.

He retired in June of 1989 as senior partner of a four-man urological office. Bill thoroughly enjoyed his private medical practice for twenty-seven years. But the years since have not become "the easy life," nor did he intend for them to be.

When at home in Cape Girardeau, Missouri, most mornings Bill meets individually with men he is discipling, helping them grow spiritually. He has served on the National Board of Directors for the Christian Business Men's Committee of USA, which requires approximately four weeks a year of his time. He also is active in the CBMC ministry in Cape Girardeau, and has coordinated six "Dad, the Family Shepherd" weekend men's conferences in his city.

Only recently, Bill stepped down from the national board of the Christian Medical and Dental Society.

Last, but clearly not least, he and his wife, Eloise, regularly schedule time to visit with their four children and their families. Since only one daughter still lives in Cape Girardeau (the others live in Fayetteville, North Carolina, Albuquerque, New Mexico, and Des

Moines, Iowa), this means considerable travel in addition to annual family get-togethers.

If this range of activities doesn't fit the standard "retirement" mold, Bill offers no apologies.

"Several months ago, Eloise and I went for a drive between sessions of a CBMC meeting we were attending in California. At one point, we noticed there were large golf courses on both sides of the highway in this well-known retirement area. All we could see were golfers and their carts," he says.

"For some reason, we wondered how many of those men viewed golf as *the priority* in their lives. One day, they will die, someone will take their place in their foursome, and the game will go on.

"That is not my idea of productive use of retirement years. There's nothing wrong with golf or any other form of recreational activity (I prefer tennis), but it's not *the priority* for me."

Bill has strategically planned and worked through a series of personal goals that he established through much prayer twelve years ago, planning ahead for his retirement—and a shift from part-time to full-time lay ministry.

"I was fortunate enough to be able to retire while still relatively young in life. I wanted my post-career years to count for eternity. I used to think taking out a kidney or a prostate would be the most exciting thing I'd ever do in this life, but today I'd have to revise that. To paraphrase the eloquent words of King Solomon so many years ago, the only worthwhile pursuit in this life is knowing and serving God (Eccles. 12:13).

"So I have determined to invest the gifts and abilities God has given me, as a layman, in pursuits that will help to point people toward Jesus Christ."

*Submit to one another
out of reverence for Christ.*

—Ephesians 5:21

Taming the Tension

Balancing work and family demands

*B*uilding a successful family is much harder than building a successful career. A career requires the investment of time and talent, but not necessarily sacrifice if you enjoy what you're doing. A strong family life, however, cannot be achieved without sacrifice, since it often calls for doing those things that are not exciting: taking out the trash; refereeing sibling squabbles; paying bills; walking the dog in the rain; cleaning out the refrigerator; fixing a leaky toilet.

When men (and increasingly, women) have family problems, the temptation is to immerse themselves in work, performing tasks they like and feel good doing, while avoiding unpleasantness in the home, where they feel inadequate. "Ignore the bad and maybe it will go away" is the motto that some follow. These make up a sizable portion of the workaholic population.

Corporation job descriptions are often clear-cut. We know when we're doing well. But family job descriptions are seldom so sharply defined. They also have an annoying tendency to undergo revision—without our knowing it. Just when you think you have married life figured out, babies start arriving. And children grow up. Before you can master one phase, they have shifted into another. *Why bother?* we think in frustration. *I'll just work hard, earn a good paycheck, and take the path of least resistance.*

This is not the option, however, for Christians in business. We are admonished to provide for the material requirements of our families, but the Bible also exhorts us to address the emotional and spiritual needs of spouse and children. The question is, "How?" Who can worry about family obligations when, with our work schedules already overloaded, the supervisor shows up with a new assignment and says, "You aren't doing anything between 2 and 3 A.M., are you?"

It's a challenge, but we can't effectively represent Christ in the workplace if our family lives are neglected. How to achieve the needed balance is the focus of this section.

Chapter 28

A Question of Balance

Schedule versus family

Skip Johnson

(Editor's Note: Skip Johnson's a busy man: executive vice-president with Provident Bankshares Corporation in Baltimore, Maryland, and group manager-administration for Provident Bank of Maryland, heading six divisions for the forty-two-branch commercial bank. He serves on the board of directors for United Way of Central Maryland, as well as several other community boards; is active in his church; and serves as a leader for the Christian Business Men's Committee in downtown Baltimore.

Despite these many demands, he maintains only a forty-two-and-a-half-hour work week to ensure both quality and quantity time with his wife and three daughters. He explains how in the following story.)
///

Often in preparing for a workshop, you become your own best pupil. That's what happened to me a few years ago while preparing to give a session on time management at a Christian businessmen's conference.

Taking Control

I have always been a firm believer in time management and have taken several courses on the subject. But in planning my own workshop, I realized that I was still breaking a cardinal rule of time management—allowing other people to dictate much of my own schedule. Worst of all, my family was suffering the consequences.

When I came back from the conference, I resolved to make some changes. One important step was to put my calendar on the computer, scheduling such details as opening mail and returning phone calls. I determined to manage the use of my time the same way I manage my finances. There's not enough of either to go around, and everybody wants some of it, so it's up to me to determine how my time—as well as my money—is spent.

I asked my wife, Rosemary, when she felt it most important for me to be at home with the family. It was important to her to have us all together for dinner—6 P.M. at the latest. My routine had been to get home from work between 6:30 and 7:00, so I resolved to leave for work thirty to sixty minutes earlier.

To do this meant changing my work schedule, reporting to the office earlier each day, working an eight and a half hour day (8 A.M. to 5:30 P.M.), five days a week. When people ask how many hours I work in an average week, without hesitation I respond, forty-two and a half hours. This may sound unusual with fifty-, sixty-, and even seventy-hour work weeks the standard for many business executives, but it's a commitment I needed to make—and God has honored it.

My philosophy is simple: While I'm at work, I work. When I'm away from work, I do other things.

This doesn't mean I am inflexible. When dealing with a tight time frame or crucial deadlines, I adjust—but that usually means going in earlier as opposed to staying later. On *very rare* exceptions, I stay beyond 5:30, but generally other employees at the bank can set their watches by me—at half-past five, I'm headed for the elevator.

One other exception might be taking home one or two hours of work during a real crunch period, but this doesn't happen more than once a week. And I make certain not to deal with it until I have spent time with Rosemary and the kids. Even then, if Rosemary needs me, I'm available—I never shut the door.

Since my involvement with CBMC and several community organizations also takes time, I try to accomplish as much as I can at breakfast meetings before work, or over lunch. Rosemary would rather I leave home early than stay at work late; mornings are hectic with our two older daughters, Michelle and Rachel, getting ready for school. At night they are more relaxed and enjoy reading Bible stories, playing, and talking about their day.

Planning what I do well in advance is critical to achieving my objectives. It's not unusual for me to schedule luncheon meetings with people three to four weeks in advance. Those dates come up more quickly than you realize.

Weekends are for family time. Rosemary and I try to go on dates at least every other weekend, and I aim for time—just the kids and me—on a regular basis. Recently, for example, Rosemary enjoyed an afternoon to herself while the girls and I went to a soccer game. We all had fun.

A critical element in my approach to balancing time between work and family, however, is prayer. Since deciding not to leave my family only the leftovers of my time, I have learned the truth of 1 Thessalonians 5:17, which says, "Pray without ceasing" (NASB). I start each day at home with prayer, praying also on the way to work, throughout my workday, on the way home, and conclude the day with prayer.

Reliance on Prayer

I believe that every decision, challenge, and activity during the day should be committed to prayer. God's wisdom and guidance are essential for sorting through the demands of a businessperson's day, helping us to distinguish the essential from the urgent.

Proverbs is one of my favorite books of the Bible. These passages remind me that Christians should focus, ultimately, not on results and outcomes, but on doing a good day's work and being a strong, positive witness for Christ. Results and outcomes are up to the Lord, as it states in Proverbs 16:9, "In his heart a man plans his course, but the Lord determines his steps."

Acting in Faith or in Fear?

Several years ago, the Lord put my commitment not to overemphasize my job to the test. A new CEO had just been appointed. Even though I was one of the top-ranking bank officers, I would basically have to prove again my worth to the organization. A lot of people increased their work schedule to fifty to sixty hours out of fear, and I admit feeling the same temptation. But I decided just to continue doing my job as efficiently and effectively as I could and let my work speak for itself.

At my year-end performance review, my boss said he was very pleased with my work. I asked his opinion of my fixed, predictable work schedule, since he typically worked more hours. He responded that all he cared about was my getting the job done, and done well. Since he felt I was doing both, my 8:00 to 5:30 workday didn't bother him.

According to an old saying, if you want something done, find a busy person to do it. That's a trap I could easily fall into, so Rosemary serves as my sounding board. We talk and pray about all requests I receive. Unless we both agree, I don't accept. It is hard sometimes, but to maintain priorities you sometimes must say no.

Recently I drafted a detailed purpose statement for my life. This has proved helpful, not only for setting overall direction, but also as a filter for weighing new opportunities. If one fits into an aspect of my life where I need to do better I will accept. But if it falls into an area where I already feel I'm doing what God wants of me, I turn it down. You can do too good a job, adversely affecting others areas of your life.

It's all a matter of balance.

Priorities for the Long Term

Discovering the vital relationship between priorities and time management led to the turning point of Skip Johnson's life.

I was attending graduate school at Loyola College at night, while working full time at a bank. One evening, a professor gave us an exercise in goals and objectives. He provided a list of twenty possible goals and twenty related activities, then asked us to rank each goal and each activity independently, in order of personal priority. The purpose was to show us that an objective's true importance is measured not by whether you believe in it, but where it falls in your priorities.

The words *eternal life* were near the bottom of the list he gave us. I had gone to church as a boy, and although I had fallen away from the church as I grew up, I still believed in God and the Bible. Being a good manager, it made sense to me to make *eternal life* my number one objective, since it was the only true long-term priority.

But comparing that objective with activities in my life, I saw a great disparity between what I felt was important and where my time was spent. When I left class, I determined to pursue my objective of eternal life with earnest.

That was in 1978. Several years later, Skip met some men involved with CBMC who helped him discover that Jesus Christ is the only way to achieve the objective of eternal life.

Since that time, I have seen the benefits of learning God's point of view regarding the other priority areas of my life—including family and business—and following His standard, rather than my own.

Chapter 29

A Picture-perfect Relationship

Avoiding conflict between business and marriage

Robert J. Tamasy

Jim Mathis is one husband who doesn't have to call his wife when he needs to work late. And she never feels threatened by the woman he works with every day. It's just never a problem—because the woman Jim works with *is* his wife, Louise.

Partners in marriage since 1971, Jim and Louise became partners in business in 1976. Jim had established Mathis Photo, a black-and-white custom photography lab in Overland Park, Kansas, in 1973. When growth of the business required a second person, he offered the job to Louise.

"I needed someone to help me. Since Louise wasn't happy in her job as a life insurance underwriter, I asked her to work with me. She agreed—after I convinced her I could afford to pay her."

The decision turned out to be one of the best they ever made. "We get along very well together," Jim says. "We see the business as a partnership, with management and business decisions carried out jointly."

Strengths Complement

Since they have different personal strengths and interests, Jim and Louise complement each other in the business. She is a better judge of people, which is an asset in screening prospective clients, and he has more technical expertise, which he uses in evaluating equipment and supplies.

They have a general "division of labor," in which Jim develops film, shoots copy negatives, makes large prints (8x10 and larger) and contact proofs, while Louise does smaller prints and reprint orders. They share other duties, such as answering the phone, talking with customers, and doing housekeeping chores around the shop.

"After nearly eighteen years, I can't imagine not working with Louise. The business would be a real drag without her," Jim states. "Occasionally we have to work late on a special project, so we can go out for pizza and then return to the shop. But we try not to make a habit of it."

Striking a Balance

Since they don't have children, Jim and Louise have more flexibility than couples in business together who have families, but they still see the importance of striking a balance between the vocational and personal sides of their lives.

"Although we probably spend more time together than many married couples, we're not twins or clones," Louise points out. "We have our own interests. For instance, I'm very active as an officer in my national sorority, Kappa Delta, and in the church women's ministry, while Jim spends a lot of non-working time as a leader of the Christian Business Men's Committee. But we spend enough time together that we can agree if we need to do things separately in the evening."

Nevertheless, balancing the demands of business and marriage requires Jim and Louise to do careful planning.

"I don't think our challenges in maintaining balance in our lives are much different from couples who don't work with one another," Jim says. "We still have to plan time together, away from the business. We try to have a date together once a week and, while it's not a rigid rule, we try to avoid shop talk.

Quality Time Away from Work

"Couples we know who work together often struggle because they don't make a commitment to spending good time together apart from the business, doing fun things."

Their photo lab is only open Monday through Thursday. This allows Jim and Louise to take advantage of long weekends, taking bicycling and snow skiing trips, going to the Ozark mountains and theme parks. Their dates together include attending theatrical plays, films, museums, antique shows, and—one concession to the business—camera shows.

"There is an old saying that if you don't plan your time, someone will plan it for you," Jim says. "That's true for us. We're planners anyway, so we enjoy planning and looking forward to special times together. Regardless of what kind of job you have, there is always too much work to do, so if you don't plan nonwork activities, you won't do them.

Too Important to Miss

"Louise has more to do than I, since she does most of the housework, too. I help as much as I can, but we have found it necessary to schedule date nights. Those are too important for us to miss."

Their planning process, according to Louise, is kept as simple as possible. During the holidays, at the end of each year, they schedule the major activities during the upcoming year.

"Then, once a month, we check the calendar to see what we have going on and determine how we will use the free time we have left," she says. "We try to save Friday nights for ourselves, but if that doesn't work, we just set aside another evening. It's good to plan, but we realize the need to be flexible."

Chapter 30

Corporate Nomads

Moving family for the sake of career

Rick Griffith

Growing up, I experienced firsthand what it means to live in the rat race. By the time I entered ninth grade, I was attending my ninth school.

My father worked with a major corporation, always taking the next best job to advance his career. Before he could find the end of his rainbow, he was "forced out," largely due to his increasing dependency on alcohol to handle the stress. This quest virtually decimated our family; my father and mother were divorced in the mid-1970s.

After graduating from Texas A&M University in 1979, I began working in corporate environments. I was hired as a clinical engineer with DuPont, but two years later turned down a promotion to become a design engineer in Wilmington, Delaware. I was more interested in marketing, and after living most of my life in the South, a move to the East Coast was not appealing.

Instead, I accepted a position with IBM, which was my employer from 1981 to 1992. IBM, many corporate veterans will tell you, stands for "I've Been Moved," and I experienced some of that—beginning with Kansas City, then transfering to Dallas, then finally on to Oklahoma City. Fortunately, in the late 1980s IBM began to temper its relocation policy, recognizing the tremendous cost—both to the individual and the corporation—of moving people every two years or so. So at the "wise old age" of thirty-five, I took a detour from the career path my father followed.

Taking New Consulting Role

IBM's decision to create more than sixty trading areas across the United States established a network of jobs so that promising staff personnel could gain additional training and experience without having to move from region to region. After nearly five years in various management roles, I started 1992 as a business partner consultant with IBM, assisting and advising small businesses that are vital to our ongoing success. Since 1987, Oklahoma City has remained home for me and my family—something that was virtually unheard of within IBM a decade ago.

Not that transfers from one area to another in IBM had become passé. In 1990 I turned down a job offer within the company to move to Chicago. In 1991 I asked that my name be taken out of consideration for a position in Dallas when I learned it would require spending 85 percent of my time traveling. I could have utilized my university training in biomedical engineering with the Dallas job, but with four children under the age of seven, I felt it would better for me not to spend most of my time on an airplane.

Two factors over the last several years caused me to reevaluate the course of my career. Even though I had suffered through the rigors of frequent relocations as a youngster, my life was also in the classic "two years and move" cycle.

Would They Do It Again?

The first factor was getting to know six men who, about fifteen years earlier, had been exactly where I was. Each was in his late forties or early fifties, and had gone through repeated transfers around the country until the mid-1980s, when IBM had a major reorganization, putting an end to their corporate ladder ascent.

I had lunch with each man, one by one, and asked him to tell me honestly whether he thought the frequent moves had been worthwhile—would he do it over again if he could? Not one of them said yes. Most of them were divorced, largely due to stresses of the job, and were trying to be more successful with a second family. They were typical workaholics, giving sixty to seventy hours a week to the job, feeding their so-called "Type A" personalities. I could identify with them because that is my tendency, too.

The thought kept coming to me, *Not one of them would do it over again!*

Observations of a King

Their comments reminded me of King Solomon, who wrote the Book of Ecclesiastes, and whose life is recounted in 1 Kings and 2 Chronicles. Here was a man who had more wealth and fame than any other man in history. The Bible calls him the wisest man in the world. Yet, his continual striving to acquire more riches, power, and experiences left him miserable.

At the close of an incredible lifetime, this is what Solomon wrote: "Here is the conclusion of the matter: Fear God and keep his commandments, for this is the whole duty of man" (Eccles. 12:13).

Another factor was a simple comment I happened to hear on a Christian radio station while on a business trip. The speaker pointed out that we always manage to do what is really important to us. I thought about this as it related to my commitment to be a better father for my children than the examples I had seen at the time.

Learning from Other's Mistakes

It has been said that we must learn from our own mistakes. This is true, but we don't have to make *all* the mistakes ourselves—we can also learn from the errors of others: men like my father (who has since renewed his relationship with God and has been able to help many people through Alcoholics Anonymous), the IBM veterans who wouldn't do it all over again, and Solomon.

If it was truly important to prevent my children from joining the list of victims of corporate nomadic lifestyles, I would have to do something about it. What I did was two things:

▲ Resolve not to drag my family around the country simply for the sake of career advancement.

▲ Make my family a regular part of my daily calendar, just as I would for business or other personal appointments.

My decision not to pursue the job in Dallas came from the first commitment. And thanks to IBM's new flexibility, I was basically able to create a new job. I had been wanting to get into the consulting side of IBM, and was able to pull together the business relationships I had established over the past five years. Instead of spending 85 percent of my time on the road, I need to travel only about 15 percent.

I have a theory that if both mom and dad are with the children at breakfast, they can have a great impact on how the kids approach their day. Our children are too young to see how this theory will turn out, but I view it as an important investment.

Several years ago, we realized another benefit: Our newborn daughter, Lauren, developed a viral infection that required her to spend several days in the hospital when she was only three weeks old. My new responsibilities enabled me to work out of my home, playing "Mr. Mom" for our three older children while my wife, Allison, stayed with Lauren.

Obviously, if I had no alternative, I would accept a transfer or a job requiring a lot of travel rather than fail to provide for my family. But thankfully, that issue hasn't presented itself. For me, the issue was much more simple: Was I going to go the way of men like my father, who achieved high six-figure incomes but lost their families in the process, and Solomon; or would I choose to be the husband and father God wants me to be? My choice will be my family every time.

As Patrick Morley points out in his book, *The Man in the Mirror,* no one has ever won the rat race. I'm going to continue trying to be the best employee I can possibly be, but I've got to give top priority to God, and then my wife and children. That's a race I know I can finish—and win!

The Myth and Mistake of Irreplaceability

Sometimes people sacrifice time with their families because they feel "irreplaceable" at work. This is both a myth and a mistake, according to Rick Griffith.

In business, the "gotta do's," those "imperatives" that *must* be done right now, can cause us to miss the truly important. Often things that seem so imperative really aren't. If you set them aside and let them simmer, frequently they just go away.

We can't do it all. In a large corporation, there's always more work than anyone can do, so the trick is to concentrate on what's important. In physics we learn that a gas will occupy as much space as you give it. Imperatives in business are like that: If you only schedule three hours of important things, the imperatives—the seemingly urgent—will fill the remainder of your work day.

The worst part of it is, if we spend our time dealing with the imperatives we might be replaced by someone who understands how to emphasize the important. Ultimately, we're measured only by the important stuff—the bottom line—so it makes sense to leave the imperatives for somebody else.

The mistake of feeling irreplaceable, according to Rick, is that it can erect a barrier to career advancement.

If you make yourself indispensable to attain job security, you may find that the company really can't do without you where you are—so you get passed up when a opportunity to advance comes along. You may indeed become secure where you are, but if you want to move, you're stuck.

In the past eight years, I have had five jobs, all promotions. I'm not the smartest or brightest person in the company, but I made myself promotable. I learned my jobs and did them well, but made certain that I wasn't the only person who could do them. I split the workload with other people who could perform it as well as I did, so my superiors could feel confident that when I moved up, my job would still get done.

She considers a field and buys it. . . .
She sets about her work vigorously;
her arms are strong for her tasks.

—Proverbs 31:16, 17

Especially for Women in Business

*W*ith eighteen thousand women holding elected offices in local, state, and national governments, it's hard to believe that just over seventy years ago, women didn't even have the right to vote. And today, there are approximately 60 million women in the work force—more than 40 percent of the total.

In the 1980s, women affirmed their place in the American business community as never before. The decade has been termed the "decade of women in leadership." Millions of men report to women bosses. Business careers became bonafide options—or additions—to the traditional roles of child raising and homemaking.

But the surge of women into the workplace has brought with it a new set of issues, resulting in part from the different perspectives and needs that they bring with them. An intense period of adjustment has been required, and still continues, as men and women sort through the marketplace ramifications of what the French term, *vive la différence*.

Experts assert that the differences between men and women are not confined to Biology 101. For example, women are demonstrating new ways of managing people and solving problems. They emphasize "connecting" with others and building consensus—utilizing their typically stronger relational skills—instead of holding to traditional chains of command. In fact, business authorities regard Japanese management theory, which has dramatically affected management styles through information sharing and 100 percent participation, as feminine in approach. Without question, this fresh, new focus—we could call it a paradigm shift—has fostered countless benefits for the modern business world.

But these gains have not come without drawbacks. While men have spent time adjusting to the increased involvement of women in a once male-dominated environment, women have also had to rethink their roles. For instance, they have had to address serious questions of personal priorities. Is it possible for them to "have it all," to be the "superwomen" who deftly juggle home and office responsibilities without breaking into a sweat? Some can, others cannot. For those in the latter category, this means a moment of decision when they must determine priorities and make difficult choices.

In the following section, women—and men—offer their insights into one of the most important issues of the day.

Chapter 31

The Superwoman Complex

An Interview with Mary Whelchel

Robert J. Tamasy

When discussion turns to women in business, Mary Whelchel knows the territory well. A twenty-year veteran of the workplace wars, Mary currently heads her own business training company, specializing in sales, telemarketing, and customer service.

She also understands the businesswoman's world from another perspective—that of a single parent, having raised one daughter while managing her multi-faceted career. A "Jacqueline of many trades," Mary also maintains her "Christian Working Woman" radio ministry, based in Chicago, which airs on nearly three hundred stations across the U.S. and in other countries. She has written two books, The Christian Working Woman *and* Common Mistakes Singles Make, *and writes a regular column for* Today's Christian Woman *magazine.*

In the following interview, she discusses the unique challenges and struggles women face in the American marketplace of the 1990s.

/ / /

How are women being accepted in business today, compared to five or ten years ago? Is progress being made?

Whelchel: I wouldn't call it a lot of progress. Reports from the Department of Labor indicate there is still a "glass ceiling" for women—there aren't a lot of upper-level women managers. When I was in corporate management, our opinions and ideas weren't given very serious consideration. We have certainly made progress, but there is still not equal opportunity in the sense of attitude.

Years ago, there was a lot of talk about women searching for their identity. Is this still the case today?

We're seeing a slow coming back of the pendulum. Women's attitudes toward work are changing. Many who were led to believe they couldn't be worthwhile without a career are saying, "Wait a minute. I forfeited a lot for this career and I don't think it was worth it," and going back to traditional roles—feeling proud of it instead of guilty.

Increasing numbers of women, Christian and secular, are deciding they don't have to prove their worth by being career women. They are saying, "I can choose my role. It can be career, family, or both." We were fed a lot of garbage about fulfillment and satisfaction in jobs, and were disillusioned when it didn't come through.

Men have the same disillusionment; they just don't make as big a deal about it. They go into careers with great expectations, hit their own ceilings, and say, "Hey! This isn't everything it was supposed to be." The same thing applies to the woman who thinks she can stay home and be totally fulfilled. When we put our confidence in anything aside from Jesus Christ, we eventually find it doesn't work.

In your book, The Christian Working Woman, *you summarize the plight of the contemporary woman as the "superwoman complex." Explain what you mean.*

Thirty years ago, when the feminist movement started, women took on careers, but didn't drop any of their other hats—the "mother hat," the "female hat," the "wife hat," the "Christian hat." Statistics show women still carry the major responsibility in the home. The only real difference is that men *will* go shopping now.

Women have tried to do everything men were doing, and more, and that is an invitation to failure and frustration—trying to be a superwoman. I find most working moms carry a ton of guilt around. They feel they can't perform either of their roles to perfection and are shortchanging both.

Why do women take on so much?

Women, in general, have a tendency to want to please, so we jump through a lot of hoops, trying to make bosses, husbands, and children all happy. We have come a long way, but it's still a part of the daily routine for most of us. There are some things we can't do, even if we wanted to.

In my mother's generation, a woman was judged by the kind of house she kept and whether her children looked perfect all the time. Today, we try to do all that—which took full time—add to it a career, and end up with the "superwoman complex."

News reports indicate some women are giving up their business careers, electing to raise families. What has brought this about?

It's another example of the pendulum starting to shift in the other direction. Women who have gotten to where they wanted to be in business are asking, "What about my family and all the other things that are important to me?"

Many of them, now in their early forties, are panicking, fearing it's too late for a family. Women's biological clocks are ticking and they don't want to miss out.

Enough years have passed for this to catch up with us. It's not going to go back to where it was, but a lot of women and companies will get more creative with in-home work, part-time work, and more flexible schedules. One of my ministry's board members is a high-powered lawyer. When she had her daughter at thirty-seven years of age, never having had any children, she worked out a deal with her law firm to work three days a week.

She didn't want to leave her career, but she wasn't going to give it full-time commitment anymore.

Instead of "I can have it all," are women now saying "I can have it all—but only in moderation"?

Women are realizing they *can't* have it all, so they have to make some hard choices. They are recognizing *nobody* has it all—you can't have the super career, be the wonderful mother, and everything else at the same time. And Christians have higher priorities, along with the wonderful ability to choose based on God's principles, which give us eternal significance.

What do men need to understand most about women in the business environment?

Christian working men—and women who don't work outside the home—need to be careful about what they say and how they say it, so they don't lay guilt trips unnecessarily on women who have to work. Often I have heard well-meaning Christians talking about how important it is for mothers to stay home. I probably didn't disagree with what was said. But as a single mom, something inside of me would wrench as I thought, *I can't stay home, but my child is going to suffer because I have to work.* A lot of moms really don't have to work, but many do. Most would tell you that if they could afford to stay home they would. I've heard people say, "Now, if you're a single working mom, this doesn't apply to you." But as long as we hear it, it applies to us. Somehow, we have to speak our convictions concerning working mothers without laying guilt trips.

What about traditionalists who cling to the adage, "A woman's place is in the home"?

Look at the Proverbs 31 woman. I'm convinced she was just a description of an ideal woman. But there she is, in real estate and the manufacturing business. She had to be away from her home a considerable amount of time just to conduct those two elements of her business. She worked day and night, it says, and she looked after her household. A lot of traditional Christians hold her up as the way we are supposed to be. Well, they better take another look at the career woman. She certainly had two careers outside of homemaking. So I don't think the Bible gives room to condemn a mother or a woman who has a career—we have to get our priorities straight, fathers as well as mothers. It's no more okay for a man to neglect his family than it is for a woman.

As a career woman yourself, how have you been received?

Often, in the presence of Christian men who have strong feelings about women in the home, I feel an unspoken, judgmental attitude of, "Oh, you're a career woman. Well, you can't be very spiritual." But that is changing.

We have taught in the Christian evangelical community that the stay-at-home woman is the one who's made the right choice, and therefore must be the most spiritual. In the Scriptures, however, we see God using women who were very career-oriented, like Deborah and Esther. Not all the women were, but some were, so there's room for some of us in the business world. I give a talk called, "God Doesn't Make Cookie-Cutter Christians." He needs *all* kinds because there are all kinds of people out there who have to be reached.

I'll never forget the day I realized that it was okay to be the way God made me. I lived my first thirty years thinking I was some kind of female fluke, that women aren't supposed to be entrepreneurial, take-charge types. Then I realized God didn't make a mistake. He needs women like me. He may not need a whole bunch, but He does need some.

I keep going back to Matthew 6:33. We are to seek first God's kingdom and His righteousness. If we do that, the Lord will direct as He sees fit.

The Overworking Woman

I think working women are very prone to finding themselves in the predicament of being overworked, overcommitted, tired, and exhausted. A lot is expected of us. Many of us not only hold down demanding jobs, but run a household as well. We have husbands, and children, and housework, and all that they demand. Some of us are single mothers, and do all that work without anyone at home to help share the responsibility. And those of us who are single often have the responsibility for aging parents, as well as our home and various outside activities.

— Mary Whelchel, *The Christian Working Woman,* Old Tappan, N.J.: Fleming H. Revell Co., 1986.

Chapter 32

A Woman's Place Is in the . . . ?

An attorney's choice between career and family

Susy Downer

When I was twelve years old, I decided I wanted to be a lawyer. That was in 1962, long before that role became fashionable for women, but I never deviated from my goal. Through high school and then college, my eyes remained focused on the prize of a law degree and the career that would follow.

I met my husband, Phil, at Southern Methodist University in Dallas. We fell in love and began talking about marriage. Other guys I had dated didn't take my aspirations seriously, but Phil even started talking about going to law school with me. We married in 1971, following our junior year of college, and began applying to law schools.

After being accepted at several, we chose to enroll at Emory Law School in Atlanta. Our goals were realized in 1975 when we received our degrees and began the practice of law. Phil was hired by a law firm, while I joined the corporate law department of Delta Air Lines.

Being a lawyer was everything I had imagined; I absolutely loved my job. Handling a variety of corporate legal problems, I was responsible for lawsuits in major cities around the United States. This necessitated just enough travel to make it exciting.

The Ideal Job

In 1979 I was promoted to assistant corporate secretary to Delta's board of directors, making me the airline's only woman officer. My career could not have been more fulfilling—I used to say I would do my job for free, I loved it so much.

But while my educational and career paths had been smooth, our marriage had been extremely rocky. Only through God's intervention did Phil and I stay together. We were close to divorce in 1976 when we both gave our lives to Jesus Christ, largely through the Christian Business Men's Committee ministry. As the Lord began making changes in our lives, He also started to put our marriage back together. For me, that included gaining a new love for Phil to replace the love that had died over our first five years of marriage.

A New Priority

Up to that point, we had little interest in children. Our careers always took first priority. As we observed CBMC families in Atlanta and at Christian conferences, however, we began to want children, too.

Our first daughter, Abigail, was born in 1981. I couldn't believe how much fun it was to be a mother. We hired a wonderful woman to stay in our home with her while I returned to my job. I would get up early to play with Abigail before going to work, and most days I would rush home at lunch to spend another thirty minutes with her before returning to the office for the afternoon. This seemed to work out very nicely.

As much as I loved that precious baby, I also cherished my job. I had become accustomed to the salary, stock bonuses, and many benefits, including virtually free flights to most parts of the world. We enjoyed the luxury of going to Disney World for a day, flying to New York City for a dinner party, and vacationing in Europe and Japan.

Role Models

While we were leading this fast-paced lifestyle, CBMC wives in Atlanta became important role models for me. Participating in Bible studies and other ministry activities in members' homes, I observed many women who had foregone career ambitions to invest their full time in children.

I could see the difference this investment seemed to be making in their families, and also thought of the example of my own mother, who had counted it a privilege to give up a career as a medical technologist to raise four happy, secure children.

Our first son, Paul, was born in 1982. As I returned to work again, I continued to have the nagging thought: *Are you really doing the best thing for your children?*

When Abigail was about two and a half, she entered the stage of asking one question after another in a never-ending stream. One day at work, while considering this, a thought occurred to me: *Who is answering Abigail's questions this morning?* Of course, it was our housekeeper. As wonderful as she was, I knew she wouldn't answer every question the way I would.

"God, What Do You Want?"

Finally, I mustered the courage for a single, feeble prayer. "God, will You please make me want to do what You want me to do?" Over time, God answered that prayer—He changed what I wanted to do, just as it says in Philippians 2:13. "For God is at work within you, helping you want to obey him, and then helping you do what he wants" (TLB).

My heart, which had been set on a challenging, rewarding law career, changed to longing to stay at home with my children. I decided to leave my job in 1985, after Matthew was born. The decision surprisingly was not difficult. My salary and benefits would be left behind, but I was excited to give the best part of every day to my husband, children, and my personal ministry with other women.

Focusing on the Eternal

It amazes me that I have not once missed my job with Delta. (There have been times, though, when I have missed my secretary!) I traded a temporal challenge of trying lawsuits for the eternally significant challenge of raising godly children.

Years ago, Phil and I committed together to make as significant an impact as we could on this world for the Lord Jesus Christ. I remember the day when it occurred to me how much greater our impact would be if we could pass on this vision to each of our children, and their love for Christ could be multiplied through the lives of others. This, rather than corporate success, became our new goal.

Two years after I left Delta, we had our twins, Anna and Joshua. That fall when Abigail was to start first grade, Phil and I decided to use the home school approach. This year we are beginning our eighth year of home schooling and are thankful for the opportunity to be the major influences of our children as they mature in Christ.

One summer, a friend took my children for a day so I could review books for the upcoming school year. As I sat at our dining room table, amidst a sea of books, praying about what would be best for each child, my eyes welled up with tears as an overwhelming sense of gratitude washed over me.

I thanked God again for not allowing me to miss my true calling, and for the deep assurance that I was doing that for which He created me.

Chapter 33

For Better or Worse

The pros and cons of a "mom-and-pop business"

Bea Hicks

Anyone who says it's easy for a husband and wife to work together in business has never tried it. Building a strong marriage is enough of a challenge. To work together for a livelihood at the same time, and survive, requires the grace of God.

My husband, Charley, and I can attest to this from personal experience. In 1955, after a two-year stint in the Army, he started his own independent insurance agency. There were a lot of sales my first year—our house, our car—but not much insurance. So while Charley was getting the business established, I worked in a bank to keep food on the table.

Charley kept telling me, "Give me ten years and we'll make it," but I wasn't so sure, since there was practically no salary or commissions during those first months. I would do administrative work in the evenings, and for about a year Charley worked third shift in a foundry to provide additional income after he tried to sell insurance during the day and into the early evening.

In 1958, however, our son, Gary, was born and we decided the business had reached the point where it needed a full-time office manager. So I quit my job at the bank and started handling all the details—typing policies, giving insurance quotes, collecting premiums from new clients, and answering the phone.

My mother kept Gary and our daughter, Janet, while I was at work. Charley and I would have preferred for me stay with the children full-time, but the business took both of us to keep it going.

Charley kept assuring me, "It will be okay, we'll make it." (He's the positive one.) He can sell, but he's not good at collecting money, so that became my job. We never failed to pay promptly on an account, although we had to work hard to get some of the premiums collected. And although the temptation was there during the hard times—since premiums only had to be paid within forty-five days of issuing a policy—we never used other people's money for our own needs.

It seems that to succeed together in both marriage and business, you practically need to be exact opposites. At least that was true in our case. For instance, Charley acknowledges that I am a better judge of people, and that made me a better under-writer. I would try to listen for signals that would indicate that selling a policy to someone might be a high risk, not only for ourselves, but also for the companies we represent. Charley is inclined to give people the benefit of the doubt. That might be compassionate, but can be devastating in the insurance business. So God has enabled me to be a true "helpmate" in many ways. Friends tell us, "We could never work together," but we have really been able to complement each other.

Of course, we also started out in a different era. Today, women tend to be more independent and many of them are not willing to work for no pay, as I did in the early years. But what bothered me the most was that after a full day of work, Charley would often have to be out at night making calls on potential clients.

There were times I would rebel. He would be out knocking on doors at night, instead of staying home as I felt a self-respecting husband and father should. I griped a lot, and expected maybe too much out of him, but God gave Charley a calm spirit and a gentle Christian attitude to handle my complaining. He definitely didn't have it as easy as I did, because he had to put up with me.

We both came from poor backgrounds, and our parents had instilled the virtues of hard work. Today, with the training available on raising families, we can see we shortchanged our children, but back then, the emphasis was on working hard to get ahead. We just assumed the kids would turn out okay.

Applying the Principles

An important time in our life came in 1962, when we started to understand and apply principles we had heard from the Bible for so many years. Charley had been a Christian since the age of twelve, but the Scriptures didn't have much meaning for him until he was thirty-four. Through the Christian Business Men's Committee, meeting men who were serious about their faith on a day-to-day basis, God's truth for running a business, as well as for marriage and family life, begin to hit home.

Then in 1963, while we were attending a CBMC International Convention in Indianapolis, I committed my life to Jesus Christ. Today, I would say that Charley has the stronger faith, but over the past thirty years, particularly during stressful times, we have found our relationship with the Lord to be the real glue that has held our marriage together.

It amazes me, but most people go through life without realizing that the Bible offers all the essential answers for dealing with problems in the family and in business. If it had not been for the wisdom that permeates God's Word, we probably could not have coped with the various crises we have had to face.

Crisis in Zambia

The most recent occurred in 1988. I was still working with Charley then. Our daughter and her husband, Klaus Joujan, had been serving a second term as missionaries in Zambia. On November 30, Janet and Klaus, with two of their children, two other students, and the headmaster of the school where they worked, were riding in a pickup truck. They were headed for the boarding school to pick up their two older children for the Christmas holidays.

A large truck heading in the opposite direction, on the wrong side of the road, collided head-on with the pickup, killing Klaus and the headmaster, as well as two people in the other vehicle. The children were only slightly hurt, but Janet's back was broken and her spinal cord was damaged.

Our business came to a stop as we arranged to go overseas to be at her side. Finally, her condition stabilized and on December 13, she was brought home by her mission board to the United States. Three days later, she underwent major surgery that included inserting a steel rod into her back.

Adjusting to Children Again

In all, Janet spent four months in the hospital. During that time, Charley and I took over responsibility for the children. Even after Janet was released to go to the home that we were remodeling to accommodate her wheelchair, we continued to care for our grandchildren. It's an adjustment, at the age of sixty, to get used to having young children around the house again.

Charley and I never regretted having them. In fact, it seemed like one way of trying to make amends for not having spent enough time with our own children. But it wasn't easy for any of us. Janet, a very active and strong-willed woman, had to deal both with the loss of her husband and her own disability and ongoing rehabilitation. The children had not only lost their father, but also had to adapt to a new home environment. And Gary had to learn to share some of the undivided attention he had enjoyed.

The impact on the business was considerable. Because we both concentrated most of our energy on helping Janet and her family, the agency had to take a backseat. Charley wasn't able to spend much time with the business, and I couldn't help because of my responsibilities with the grandchildren and Janet. In 1985 we had hired a very capable woman to serve as secretary, and she took over everything that we had been doing. But because Charley could only give the business part-time attention, we finished 1989 in the red.

Today, Janet continues a miraculous recovery. The doctors once said she would never walk again, but she does very well with no assistance. She drives a car without specialized equipment. After returning to the University of Tennessee at Chattanooga to earn her teaching certificate, Janet is now in her third year of teaching at a middle school. The years since the accident have been difficult, but she still hopes one day to resume mission work in Zambia.

Working and Volunteering

I returned to our business full time early in 1992, and God has blessed us by enabling the agency to rebound from our time away from it.

I'm also doing hospital volunteer work, something I began doing after Janet was progressing well in her recovery and establishing her independence. This has provided me with many wonderful opportunities to minister to other families in crisis. Many times, 2 Corinthians 1:3–4 has shown itself to be true: "The Father of compassion and the God of all comfort, who comforts us in all our troubles, so that we can comfort those in any trouble with the comfort we ourselves have received from God."

Growing Experiences

As we look back, each phase of our lives has been a tremendous experience in Christian growth. We had always enjoyed a good marriage, but the trials of the last few years have drawn us closer together than ever. When something like this happens, you have to dig a lot deeper into what you believe. I found after a lot of self-examination that there was no place else to go but to God. It's terrible that so often it takes something like our family crisis to give true meaning to life.

If we had it to do over again, would we? Our parents and I were all strongly against Charley going into business for himself, and had we known in advance what we would be facing, we probably would not have proceeded. There were times my husband felt like a doctor, or a pastor, since he was on call twenty-four hours a day. When a client needs to file a claim, he wants to talk with his agent, no matter what time it is.

But God has been good, and He has blessed us through the tough times as well as the easy. In Jeremiah 33:3, He says, "Call to Me, and I will answer you, and I will tell you great and mighty things, which you do not know" (NASB). As Charley and I look back on our life together, our family and our business, we both can say, "Lord, You've sure got that right!"

Merging Business and Marriage

Having experienced firsthand the strains and stresses of merging business and marriage, Charles and Bea Hicks have one primary word of counsel: "If you can avoid it, don't do it!" But for couples convinced their marital relationship is strong enough for the marketplace, the Hicks offer these suggestions:

▲ Start your business with the Scriptures as your rulebook and bylaws. "In particular, follow the wisdom of John 13:35: '[that] you have love for one another.' A couple cannot spend that much time together day and night unless they have a deep, sacrificial love for each other."

▲ Be prepared to fail. "Don't set your stakes too high at first, because it won't be easy. Progress will probably be very slow."

▲ Don't be afraid of working hard. "You have to understand that a new business is going to take much of your time and energy. If you can't make that commitment, don't start."

▲ Be prepared to sacrifice. "I didn't demand a lot of clothes, because we could not have afforded them. It took most of our money just to keep the business going in the early years."

▲ Don't compare yourselves to others. "You will see others who have been much more successful, but you will also have to recognize the price they paid to get there. Are you willing to pay that price?"

▲ Evaluate your respective strengths and weaknesses, your talents and gifts. "To work well together in business, in addition to marriage, you have to balance and complement each other. If you have similar strengths and weaknesses, you're in trouble from the start."

Chapter 34

Why Women Don't Think Like Men

Valuing and capitalizing on our differences

Gary Smalley and John Trent

Let's be honest, husbands: Have you ever come away from a heated discussion with your wife and said (as we have), "Why can't she just *think* like a man?" Or have those feminine characteristics, so attractive in courtship, become sources of irritation later in marriage?

We're all aware of how different God made men and women, physically and relationally. Most of us are aware that He said, "It is not good for the man to be alone" (Gen. 2:18). But was woman designed merely to provide man with companionship—or do all the differences go deeper than that?

In researching successful families across the country, we noticed certain key characteristics that were common among these families. There was a consistent willingness to make each person in the home feel extremely valuable. In addition, there was a second key to to these successful homes: *valuing the difference between men and women.*

Most people are familiar with what God said when He created woman: "I will make [him] a helper suitable for him" (Gen. 2:18). The Hebrew word for *helper* actually means "completer." The word throughout the Old Testament talks about God being our "helper," who "completes what is lacking" or "does for us what we cannot do for ourselves."

One of the things successful husbands realize is that God created wives to complete them in important areas. A wife is designed to bring strengths to relationships that the husband does not naturally have himself. For example, here are three strengths almost every woman has that a man can wisely be thankful for—or foolishly resent:

Women encourage us to speak a "language of the heart." Do you want to lower your blood pressure? Reduce risk of heart attack? Add days to your life? The medicine we're talking about has been clinically shown to do all these things and more: meaningful communication. Typically, men spend their days speaking in factual, nonemotional, detail-oriented conversations. Most men easily speak a "language of the head." So when the average man runs out of facts to talk about, he stops talking!

But the average woman doesn't restrict her talk to facts. Most women are much more in touch with feelings, needs, dreams, and fears, and are able to talk about them on an emotional basis—the "language of the heart." This ability to share deep feelings is directly linked to good health.

In the home, a woman provides constant encouragement to share at a deep level—feelings, needs, and hurts. What many men don't realize is that by sharing both facts and feelings— deepening communication skills—not only does physical health improve, but they are *four times more likely* to receive a promotion at work!

Women press for emotional closeness, not distance. There is a deep need in most women not only for meaningful communication, but also for emotional closeness and attachment. How strong is this need? One indication is that in this country alone, more than 10 million romance novels will be purchased this year—97 percent by women. Why? In part because these stories offer a picture of closeness and intimacy that, unfortunately, many women frequently find missing in their own lives.

The average man is more comfortable with distance in a relationship. While emotional distance can help in working things out at "arms length" at work, that natural tendency can work against him at home.

A proverb states, "He who separates himself from others quarrels against all sound wisdom." Being wise in God's eyes involves closeness. Christ modeled it with the disciples, and a wise husband will allow his wife to be his "close companion," as it calls for in Song of Solomon.

Women will personalize their world. Most women become personally involved in their environment. They often give names to cars, fill rooms and offices with pictures, care deeply for the family pet, and feel attacked if you criticize the wallpaper they have picked out. ("But honey, I wasn't criticizing you. I was criticizing the wallpaper!")

Men view things around them as either functional or not—clothes, cars, furniture, or whatever. Do they work, or not? Women view things around them as extensions of themselves. What they drive, where they live, how their homes are decorated, what they wear, are all extensions of the persons that they are.

This sensitivity can make it easier for a woman to spot emotional hurts in children, or sense when "something has changed." A wise man views her ability to perceive differences in another's world as a blessing to help identify and head off problems, not a characteristic for ridicule or attack.

Differences between men and women are neither wrong nor right. Just *different.*

So we fix our eyes not on what is seen,
but on what is unseen.
For what is seen is temporary,
but what is unseen is eternal.

—2 Corinthians 4:18

Going Over the Edge

Sailing out on faith

In fourteen hundred and ninety-two,
  Columbus sailed the ocean blue;
  In the nineteen hundred and nineties, too,
  Modern-day people take risks. They do!

We can almost imagine the conversation:

"Chris, you're crazy. Everyone knows the world is flat! You'll sail right off the edge!"

"We don't *know* that! In fact, it says in an old book that the earth is round. I'm sailing west, and no one is going to stop me."

"You're a fool—an empty-headed risk taker! And what old book are you talking about?"

Through the ages, Christopher Columbus has been synonymous with risk taking, the idea of going boldly where no one has previously gone. What generally is not known, however, is that Columbus was less cavalier and foolhardy than we might think.

His journals reveal that old Chris was very devout in his faith. In fact, he felt God was leading him into a divine mission. He wrote, "God made me the messenger of the new heaven and the new earth of which He spoke in the Apocalypse of St. John . . . and He showed me the spot where to find it."

The "old book" he could have been referring to in the imaginary dialogue was written by the prophet Isaiah, who stated that God "sits enthroned above *the circle of the earth*" (Isa. 40:22). Christopher Columbus: wild-eyed adventurer, or faithful man diligently following a course clearly mapped out by God?

More than five hundred years after the legendary explorer's fabled voyages to the New World, risk taking remains an adventure—and an inexact science. There seems a bit of Columbus in each of us, fascinated by the prospect of living on the edge, daring to try—and even succeed at—something we have never done before. Better yet, something *no one* has ever done before! We yearn for the unpredictable, flirt with danger, court disaster—armed only with conviction that everything will turn out just fine.

But like Columbus, how can we distinguish pure risk taking from a true step of faith? How far is foolhardy? How do we separate legitimately calculated risks from "stupid moves?"

Chapter 35

Up the River Without a Paddle

Lessons of a risk taker

F. David Jenkins

On the wall in my office at home hangs an unusual collage that my wife, Barbara, gave me for Christmas. The collage is made up of thirty different business cards that I have used at one time or another during our twenty-four years of marriage.

It's a kind of portrait of my career as an entrepreneur. I have never been afraid to start something new, and when one project is completed or folds, I'm always ready for the next enterprise. It's fun bringing innovative concepts to fruition.

Some of the cards represent very successful ventures, such as being involved in the technological development for the debit card system now used in many service stations around the United States. I have also been involved with cellular phones and developing a nonionized gas detector.

But in my type of work, one thing must be understood— some ideas are not going to work. When you sit across a table from a wild-eyed inventor, scribbling his brainstorm on the back of an envelope and asking you to help in raising the three million dollars needed to build a prototype, success isn't guaranteed. A few of my business cards were for projects like these.

Of Mice and Men

This is where the risk comes in. No one can predict the future with complete accuracy. As author John Steinbeck noted, the plans of mice and men sometimes go astray.

One of my most notable failures began in 1983, not long after I had become a Christian at age forty-two. There was an opportunity to enter into a general partnership to buy a hotel in Alaska, located right along the Kenai River, the premier salmon fishing area in the world. From a business rationale, it made sense, and all the numbers seemed to work. What could go wrong?

There were three factors that did concern me: my partner was not a Christian, the hotel featured a bar, and neither of us had ever been in the hotel business. In spite of these considerations, and a general uneasy feeling, I proceeded with the deal. Almost immediately, our "risk-free, sure thing" turned into financial quicksand.

By 1987, four of us—Barbara and I, my partner and his wife (who was a believer)—had moved into the hotel in an attempt to cut expenses by replacing the nine regular employees. Over the next eighteen months that we were there, I had a total of five days off. In spite of this, we couldn't keep the riverside business afloat.

Looking back, it wasn't hard for me to determine what had gone wrong. As a new Christian, I had failed to let God be a central part of my decision. I had discounted my uneasiness simply as nervousness over engaging in an unfamiliar type of business.

As our ties to the hotel were cut in July of 1987, when the facility went into foreclosure, I wrestled with the realization of how I had thrown away all the financial resources that the Lord had entrusted to me. At my wit's end, I uttered a simple prayer: "Lord, what do you want me to do?" His answer was not audible, but clear and equally brief: "Turn it all over to Me."

Ongoing Lessons

Since then Barbara and I have been learning an ongoing lesson in how God takes care of His children when they elect to follow Him. At this writing, I am once again "in transition," having been laid off from a major corporation after three years and following that, a brief stint with a struggling computer company that went out of business. At least the employment period lasted long enough for us to get back on our feet financially while we pray about the Lord's next "assignment."

"The Tummy Factor"

In seeking His direction, I place great emphasis on two important principles about taking risks. The first is sometimes referred to as "the tummy factor." This is where I went wrong in 1983. Deep down I felt that things weren't right, even though all the facts and figures seemed to point to success. I didn't realize that God, through the Holy Spirit, was trying to tell me that I was on the verge of going up the river without a paddle.

This tummy factor, of course, is not unique to Christians. Secular business experts recognize this principle as well, although they can't always point to a specific source. They consider it instinct or a "gut feeling"; I call it divine discernment.

When I entered into the hotel partnership nine years ago, I thought my risk was in embarking on an enterprise outside my realm of experience. In fact, the risk I took was to ignore the very clear warning I was receiving from God.

"Whiz-Bang" Sensation

The second principle I have learned is that to enter into any venture without considering how—or if—it will honor God, is truly taking a risk. Often we jump at a business opportunity on the promise of financial rewards or the "whiz-bang" sensation of doing something exciting and different.

At one time, that had been my motivation, but today my perspective has changed dramatically. In Matthew 6:25, Jesus tells us, "do not worry about your life, what you will eat or drink; or about your body, what you will wear." If we are going to live in obedience to the Lord, we must take teachings like this seriously.

Recently I had an opportunity to work for two investment companies. Financially, the incentives were good. I would be able to pay off my mortgage in five years instead of ten. There is nothing inherently wrong with being in the investment business, but I had to ask if this was what God wanted *me* to do. Would this decision enable me to honor the Lord?

Objective: To Honor God

Jesus commanded us to "Seek first his kingdom and his righteousness, and all these things will be given to you as well" (Matt. 6:33). To me, this means that, as we consider the risks associated with business, our objective should be to honor the Lord. If I were to stumble across a way of turning turnips into gold, but it depends totally on me and not on God, my attitude should be "forget this project."

This is not to say that as Christians we are to avoid risks of any kind. In His parable of the talents in Luke 19, Jesus tells of a wealthy man who entrusted some of his financial resources to his servants, instructing them to put this money to work in his absence. Later, the man consulted with each servant to see how he had put the funds to work.

The ones who invested the money and received a healthy return were rewarded. One servant, however, hid the money. His very conservative decision was to hang on to what he already had, rather than risk it to gain more. That servant was severely chastised by his master.

Using Our Gifts and Resources

To me, the lesson is clear: God does not want us to act indiscriminately, but He entrusts us all with unique gifts, talents, and resources. We are to use these wisely, depending upon Him to provide clear direction on how, when, and where.

Some years ago, I came across a fascinating quote from Hudson Taylor, the noted missionary pioneer: "All of God's giants have been weak men and women who did great things for God because they counted on His faithfulness." This flies straight in the face of conventional business thinking, which generally focuses on self-reliance and maximizing your strengths while minimizing your weaknesses.

But Taylor was right. In Psalm 23, we read that God is with us through the valley of the shadow of death. There is a great difference between death and its shadow. As God leads us, we can rely on Him because He knows where all the potholes are.

As I see it, risk-taking looks a lot different to the Christian who is striving to walk consistently with the Lord. As He directs our paths (Prov. 3:5–6), we can move ahead in the confidence that He has already calculated the risks for us.

Chapter 36

Who's in Control?

Where do you turn when you don't know where you are?

Clyde Hawkins

There are two systems that pilots use for flying. One is IFR (Instrument Flight Rules), which is what the airlines use. At the airport you file a flight plan, and a few minutes later you taxi to the runway. Before you take off, you pick up the microphone and submit your complete control to the system and do exactly what they tell you to do, from the time you are ready to leave until the time you touch down on the other end.

There is a second system called VFR (Visual Flight Rules), in which you follow the rules and stay on track yourself, kind of like driving a car. Once you have cleared the traffic area around the airport, they say, "Good day. Squawk 1200 on the transponder and we'll see you." Then you are on your own.

One time I was flying toward Birmingham, Alabama, and the weather was supposed to be a one-thousand-foot ceiling and improving. I was only a VFR pilot, not instrument-rated at that time. All of a sudden, the weather that was supposed to be getting better got worse. Very quickly the clouds were what we call "in the trees," so I had to climb out.

I took my plane on top of the clouds and started checking the weather throughout the entire area. I was "socked in." There was complete cloud cover all over the Southeast, and I was flying by Visual Flight Rules on top of it. I had a problem, needless to say. It was a bad day for flying.

I had to do something, so I called the Birmingham control tower. This is something nobody likes to do, especially pilots. I had to admit that I was lost and disoriented. Flying on top of the cloud cover, I needed to get into the system. Since I was not an instrument-rated pilot in those days, this was generally not done, but the air traffic controllers in Birmingham took me right in.

They told me to head a certain direction, advised me on how quickly to descend, and instructed me on when to turn. Birmingham Airport looked awfully good when I finally broke through the clouds.

Federal Aviation Administration officials say that if those pilots who are in conditions like that, VFR in the clouds, would do one thing—just pick up the microphone and call—they could save about 50 percent of them. But most of them fly into hills, mountains, or trees, never asking for help because they're too proud. They want to control their own destination; they want to be the boss.

Anyone who has flown very much by VFR knows that eventually you are going to get caught in the clouds. If you are going to make it, you will have to pick up the microphone and ask for help.

This is true in life as well. You might make it pretty well on your own for many years, going strictly by what you see and hear, but one day there will be a point when you have to pick up the microphone and get into God's system if you're going to get in. Failure to call for His help is an invitation for disaster.

The Bible says, "And this is the testimony: God has given us eternal life, and this life is in his Son. He who has the Son has life; he who does not have the Son of God does not have life" (1 John 5:11–12). Some people may see this as narrow, but it's how God set up the system.

This is true not only for life *after* death, but also for life *before* death. Often we want to do things our own way—whether in running a business, handling our personal finances, making family decisions, or any of a number of other areas. We operate by the down-to-earth equivalent of VFR. But there are times when operating by sight just doesn't work. In fact, the Bible teaches that Christians should "live by faith, not by sight" (2 Cor. 5:7, NASB).

I believe that *every* day is a walk of faith, because there are so many unforeseeable factors, so much uncertainty. To trust solely in my own judgment is perhaps the greatest risk of all. By contrast, believing that God is all-knowing and truly desires the best for my life, committing all that I do to Him is no risk at all—it's more certain than taxes or knowing the sun will rise tomorrow morning.

So if you have never really picked up the microphone and gotten into God's system, I urge you to do so. Just as the FAA won't turn down a VFR pilot in distress, God has never turned down anyone, no matter how bad the infraction. He accepts everyone, where they are and as they are, if only they ask for His help.

But the FAA can't force a pilot to accept their assistance to guide him to safety. In the same way, because of our freedom of choice, God won't force us to accept His assistance. It's a simple matter of going through life either by VFR, not knowing what lies beyond the next corner or under the next cloud, or by IFR, getting into God's system—which happens to be the only per-fect one available.

Chapter 37

What Would You Do Differently?

Choices that affect the quality of our lives

Fred Prinzing

Editor's Note: Some years ago, a group of senior citizens were surveyed and asked, "What would you do differently if you could live your life over again?" Many of them responded, "I would take more risks." Recently, Fred Prinzing, professor of preaching and pastoral ministries at Bethel Seminary in St. Paul, Minnesota, compiled his own list of answers to that question. They are offered below for your consideration.

If I had my life to live over, I would have:

▲ watched less TV and read more books;

▲ continued my piano lessons;

▲ been less concerned with grades and more concerned with learning;

▲ dated girls with less emphasis on whether they were considered "beauties";

▲ eaten more slowly and enjoyed the conversation at mealtime;

▲ saved the marbles and baseball cards I collected;

▲ stayed home when I was sick;

▲ given more flowers while people were alive;

▲ brushed and flossed my teeth more regularly;

▲ gotten up earlier each day for my quiet time;

▲ given fewer nicknames, especially ones that hurt people;

▲ gone fishing with my sons instead of watching football on TV;

▲ listened more and talked less;

▲ watched birds;

▲ worn my hair longer (when that was still possible);

▲ attended my daughter's princess presentation instead of attending a board meeting in Chicago;

▲ been more intentional in sharing my faith;

▲ written a journal (we used to call it a diary, and only girls kept one);

▲ prayed as a first resort instead of as a last resort;

▲ left food on my plate when I was full;

▲ taken time to befriend persons with handicaps;

▲ said "Thank you," "I love you," "I'm sorry," and "Please forgive me" more often;

▲ planted a vegetable garden;

▲ enjoyed the present more, and not been so concerned about the future;

▲ tried more foods I didn't think I liked;

▲ spoken out against racial slurs and jokes;

▲ bought fewer clothes, but better quality ones;

▲ taken my kids out of school for special trips;

▲ learned to speak at least one foreign language;

▲ hugged and kissed instead of smiling and shaking hands;

▲ walked more and taken more hikes;

▲ visited shut-ins more often;

▲ learned to sew.

(Reprinted with permission from The Standard, *April 1992, published by the Baptist General Conference, Arlington Heights, Ill.)*

Chapter 38

The Dangers of Playing It Safe

Life's greatest risk is not seeking God's will

Luis Palau

When we refuse to take the risk of walking by faith in obedience to God's will and call on our life, one of the first things to go is peace of mind.

Christians in our culture have opted for the "good life." They go to church, read their Bibles, serve on church committees, and tithe. Yet none of these things, if done for their own sake, will count for eternity. When all is said and done, all that will count is whether we do the one thing God has called us to do—love Him with all our heart and soul and strength and mind.

If we love God with every fiber of our being, then we will long to be with Him. We will say with the apostle Paul, "For to me, to live is Christ and to die is gain" (Phil. 1:21).

Paul wasn't afraid to die because he knew that he had a future in heaven awaiting him. He knew, as we should know, that the exciting thing about heaven will not be the streets paved with gold, but that "the dwelling of God is with men, and he will live with them. They will be his people, and God himself will be with them and be their God" (Rev. 21:3).

Love and obedience cannot be separated. If we love God with our whole being, we will do what He calls us to do. Jesus Christ made this clear to His disciples when He said, "If you love me, you will obey what I command" (John 14:15).

What are the consequences of not heeding God's call on your life to serve Him as He intended? I found out one snowy January while preaching in Schenectady, New York.

Before the meeting started, a rather distinguished-looking gentleman with a cane entered the sanctuary, walked to the front of the church, introduced himself and asked to speak with me after the service. We arranged to meet at the home of the family with whom I was staying.

In the car on the way to their house, my hosts told me about the gentleman with the cane. "Luis," they said, "this gentleman is one of the most noted eye specialists in the country. His textbooks are studied in many major universities. He's been away from the Lord since we were in college together, but something very strong has been on his heart during the last few weeks."

A Big Decision

At the house, my hosts excused themselves so the doctor and I could talk privately for a few minutes.

"Young man," he said, "I have a question to ask you, and based on the answer you give me, I'm going to make a big decision.

"I'm an ophthalmologist. I've made a lot of money. I'm well respected. Most people think I'm a success. But my own daughter has no interest in God, and my son is going to hell because I've never shared the gospel with him. For years, I've questioned how I've spent my entire adult life. Is that success?"

He went on: "When I was in the university, a missionary by the name of John R. Mott came and spoke about the need in the Middle East for ophthalmologists to help treat eye diseases, and I felt the call of God. When Mott gave the invitation, I made a commitment to go and serve Jesus Christ on the mission field. I committed to use my medical skills for God's glory.

"But when graduation came, I married, and my friends and relatives began to warn me about the risks and dangers of living in the Middle East, the sacrifices a missionary must make, about foolishly wasting my education.

"They said, 'Don't do it,' and the pride of life got ahold of me and I never did go to the mission field. Instead, I started my own practice here in the States. That was forty-two years ago.

"And I want you to know, I haven't had one day of peace in forty-two years," he admitted. "But I'm retired now, and I have asked my wife to go to Afghanistan with me so we can finish our last days serving the Lord in mission work. I've said, 'Let's at least obey God at the end of our lives.' But she doesn't want to go. So tell me, shall I go or shall I stay?"

In typical Latin fashion, I put my arm around him and said, "Brother, I believe you should go."

He began to cry. "Thank you! I will go. God's been calling me for forty-two years. This time no one is going to stop me."

Three months later, I phoned the family I had stayed with in Schenectady. "How is the doctor doing?" I asked.

"Haven't you heard?" they replied. "He's off to Afghanistan, and his wife went with him. He's coming back to the States soon to collect medical supplies that some large companies have donated. And he's as excited as he can be."

Dying on the Outside, Alive on the Inside

The next winter I had the privilege of returning to Schenectady. The doctor was there as well. His body had grown so weak that he couldn't even stand up anymore. But he was very much alive on the inside.

"Come here," he said. "Give me one of those Latin hugs." After I greeted him, he told me, "The next time I see you, I'm going to be in the presence of the King!" A few weeks later, he went to be with the Lord.

What moved me about this doctor was the fact that for forty-two years, he had no peace because he rebelled against God's calling. When he looked back over his life, he realized that all his "great" accomplishments were worthless because he had not obeyed God's plan for his life.

As Christians, what is our supreme responsibility on this side of heaven? To be a success? Yes—but a success in God's eyes. Henrietta Mears said, "Success is anything that is pleasing to Him." I agree. We please God when we commit ourselves wholeheartedly to do whatever He calls us to do, whether that means using our talents to serve Him overseas, taking an active role ministering within our church, giving a faith-sized gift to further the Lord's work, witnessing to our family, friends, and business associates, or whatever.

It's Not Too Late

Does God have all of you there is to have? As the doctor from Schenectady discovered, it's not too late to follow God's will for your life, no matter how long you've neglected His call. It's not too late to please Him. And what a beautiful thing it is when someone finally returns to the ways of God and is prepared to enter eternity victoriously.

Are you ready to enter eternity victoriously? Are you ready and eager to do what God asks of you? Imagine the Savior saying to you, "Well done, good and faithful servant! You have been faithful with a few things; I will put you in charge of many things. Come and share your master's happiness!" (Matt. 25:21).

When all is said and done, what will the Lord say to you?

Chapter 39

What Did I Have to Lose?

A new perspective in an old book

William F. Osl Jr.

When was the last time you sat down to read an old book, one of the classics? Like most people in business, my time for discretionary reading is limited, but I can still vividly recall a time when reading one of these vintage pieces of literature literally changed my life.

In 1979 I was the head of a production shop for AT&T in Kearney, New Jersey, responsible for 225 employees and six supervisors. I was working hard, doing what most men about my age with similar positions were doing—striving to climb the corporate ladder. It seemed things were going well, and since I had been evaluated as having executive potential, the future looked very promising.

Then my wife, Stephanie, asked me an unusual question. She wanted to know if I was interested in attending a Bible study. The Bible wasn't new to me—I had learned about it through school and church activities as a young person—so I agreed.

What did I have to lose? It might even expand my intelligence, I thought. In building a career, sometimes it is the little things that can make a big difference.

In for a Shock

So we started meeting once a week with a number of couples at a church where Stephanie had been attending. To be honest, the Bible study wasn't anything like I had expected. For example, it was a shock to learn that my "normal and accepted" lifestyle wasn't pleasing to God, that it was characterized by sin—disobedience to God's laws. The good news, however, was that I wasn't unique. One passage said, "for *all* have sinned and fall short of the glory of God" (Rom. 3:23, emphasis added).

Also, for the first time I heard that it was possible to have a personal relationship with God. "For Christ died for sins once for all, the righteous for the unrighteous, to bring you to God" (1 Pet. 3:18). This was not automatic, however. It required an act of the will on my part: "Yet to all who *received* him, to those who believed in his name, he gave the right to become children of God" (John 1:12, emphasis added).

I thought about this for several weeks, finally concluding it was true, and decided to do something about it by asking God to forgive me for my sins and take control of my life. It was at this time that the Old Testament Book of Ecclesiastes helped me to put it all together.

One evening, I was sitting in my favorite chair, reading about King Solomon, whom the Bible calls the wisest man of all time. He had tried every experience, every pleasure that life can offer, and he had determined that everything is "meaningless, a chasing after the wind" (Eccles. 2:26). In the same chapter, he wrote, "A man can do nothing better than to eat and drink and find satisfaction in his work. This too, I see, is from the hand of God" (v. 24). At the end of the book he reached this conclusion: "Fear God and keep his commandments, for this is the whole duty of man" (Eccles. 12:13).

This struck home with me. Not only had I established a new relationship with God, but now I had a new perspective on my work, as well as my basic purpose in life.

The changes that began in my life were not dramatic, but they were profound. For years, I had performed well in my jobs, seeking to be recognized and rewarded for my efforts. After committing my life to Jesus Christ, climbing the corporate ladder ceased to be the driving force in my life. Just as I had given the rest of my life to God, I also yielded my professional career to Him, being willing to accept whatever He had for me.

New Motivation

Actually, this worked to AT&T's benefit, as well as my own. My motivation each day was to do the best work I was capable of doing—not for my personal satisfaction nor anyone else's, but only for God's glory. AT&T is as high quality a corporation as you will find anywhere, but God's standards of performance are even higher than anything AT&T would consider.

Since then, I have received a number of promotions, but I view these as proof of the validity of biblical principles in the work setting. I have strived to achieve a balance, maintaining an awareness that ultimately, as it says in Colossians 3:24, "It is the Lord Christ whom you serve (NASB)," but at the same time not being a flag-waver. It is much better that someone discover I am a Christian by my lifestyle and approach to my job than by my having to inform them. I don't hold myself up as a role model, but I do try to sincerely live in a way that positively reflects my commitment to God.

Need to Be Visible

When I was promoted to vice president of information management services and AT&T's chief information officer in October of 1989, I purposely chose during the first ninety days to be as visible as possible to everyone in my division. I wanted them to know about me—my job experience, why I was there, and what I saw for the future. To do that required in part that I tell something about my personal perspectives.

In addressing my spiritual beliefs, I chose to refer to God or "the Lord," but not Jesus Christ. There were two reasons for this. I felt impressed that the power of my testimony could be undermined by an insensitive, hit-'em-in-the-face approach. In addition, our organization in many respects is a crosscut of society, with people of Islamic, Jewish, Buddhist, Hindu, even atheistic beliefs.

If God provides the opportunity, I am glad to talk to anyone about what Jesus Christ has meant to me. But I feel it would be wrong to try to take advantage of my corporate position to preach to our staff and risk alienating some of them.

One of the convictions I have tried to abide by is not to sacrifice my family for my career. This is a daily struggle, and especially in a fast-paced corporate environment, it is easy to become married to a position. So I have resolved not to work weekends and make certain that I use all of my vacation time. My family deserves that. The company gets a lot out of me during the normal work week.

On the job, living out my faith can be challenging. In the mid-1980s when AT&T was going through the mandated divestiture of many of its properties, I was involved in a major downsizing over a two-year period. During that time, we went from sixteen thousand people to eight thousand.

It was partly my job to determine who would stay and who would not. Many of the people we had to let go had been with the company for a long time and had done a good job for us. It was a painful process, one that even today grabs at my emotions. You don't go through something like that without having it touch you in some way.

Looking back, I regard that as one of the most dramatic episodes of my career in shaping me as a leader and manager. It has enabled me to become more sensitive to the people who work for us, giving me a desire to be of service to them.

One of my most gratifying experiences has been serving for one year on a task force to develop a "Shared Values Statement" for our organization. This statement, which was adopted in February of 1991, expresses how we want to behave corporately and individually, and what values we cherish as an organization. Too often we focus on performance outcomes, without considering how we want these results accomplished.

Five Key Values

This statement underscores five values that we believe serve as a common bond throughout our organization:

▲ *Dignity of the individual*

▲ *Dedication to the customer*

▲ *Commitment to people*

▲ *Stewardship of AT&T's resources*

▲ *Responsibility to the larger community*

Each of these is clearly consistent with standards the Lord establishes in His Word, the Bible. Even though there seems to be strong pressure in parts of our nation to move away from biblical values, my experience is that operating according to God's guidelines, which underscore integrity, dignity, compassion, sound management, and commitment, is the only sure path to business success.

Personally, I have found prayer to be vital to carrying out my responsibilities in a way that pleases God and best serves my company. I begin each day with prayer, committing all that I do to the Lord. Then throughout the day, I apply 1 Thessalonians 5:17—"pray without ceasing"—by praying throughout the day. It may be only snippets of time, even as brief as ten seconds, but it helps me keep my focus on serving the One who matters most.

And to think it all started simply by taking the time to read an old book!

Part Eleven

Everybody's a "10"
in the Right Job / 211

Hiring: Art, Science,
or Act of Faith? / 218

Selecting the Best / 222

*Who then is the faithful and wise
manager, whom the master puts in charge
of his servants?*

—Luke 12:42

Hiring Strategies

Finding the right person for the right job

*F*or those involved in hiring people—and many of us are, to one degree or another—it would be great news to know each decision could be 100 percent assured of success. But unfortunately, that's not the case. Here are just a few of the reasons.

The process of hiring has become more difficult in recent years because of legal restrictions and because the pool of potential candidates for any given job has grown much larger.

In these days of "lean and mean" work forces, the need to match the best people possible with the right jobs is greater than ever. When staffs are pared from 600 to 350, or from 15 to 7, penalties for mistakes in judgment are multiplied. The adverse impact of wrong hiring decisions—individually and corporately—is intensified.

As Christians, we have an important stewardship, not only to our own company but also to individuals we are considering for positions on our staff team.

In addition, "delayering" and corporate cutbacks have made it necessary for more people to understand not only the steps for hiring someone, but also how to put their best foot forward when they suddenly find themselves on the other side of the hiring process—seeking new employment.

As executive placement consultant Pat MacMillan states in his interview, everyone is a "10," but only when matched with the right job. Mismatched "10s" can look alarmingly like "1s" or "2s" when assigned to roles they are ill-suited to perform.

Whether you are actively engaged in the hiring process for your company, or find yourself in the market to be hired, the information on the following pages will be of much practical value.

Chapter 40

Everybody's a "10" in the Right Job

An interview with Pat MacMillan

Robert J. Tamasy

Having talented, motivated employees is one of the joys of business. But first you must wade through the troubled and mysterious waters of the hiring process. When you have a key opening to fill, how can you be sure of finding the right person for the job?

Pat MacMillan, a business consultant in Atlanta, Georgia, acknowledges the process of sorting through a list of candidates is hard work, but it need not be a "hit and miss" approach. A division of his consulting firm, Team Resources, Inc., provides executive search services for many corporate and non-profit clients. Over the years, he and his staff have discovered hiring principles that, when violated, frequently cause a lot of trouble.

Recently, MacMillan compiled his insights into a book, Hiring Excellence *(NavPress). Many of these principles have been drawn from an unusual source, the Bible. They are found in "stories about God and His staffing strategy here on Planet Earth," he says. "Moses at the burning bush, Saul on the Damascus Road, Paul writing to*

Titus telling him how to choose elders. There are many intimations that Jesus Christ spent entire nights in prayer, but Luke 6:12 is the only place where it is stated specifically. And what did He do immediately afterward? He chose His twelve disciples. This must have been a pretty important decision for Him."

In the following interview, MacMillan discusses hiring perils and pitfalls, and offers guidelines for finding the caliber of people needed to succeed in today's turbulent, highly competitive business environment.

/ / /

From a Christian perspective, why is a proper approach to hiring so important, aside from the obvious need to find suitable individuals for various jobs?

That need is pretty important all by itself, but if everything in our possession is really God's, we are nothing more than stewards. One form of stewardship is to hire the very best people possible to help carry out the work and responsibilities God has entrusted to us. We also want to help people maximize their gifts and abilities.

The hiring process seems more complicated today. Why?

For several reasons. First, there are tremendous legal issues to consider now in making a hiring decision, such as what questions we can ask during an interview or in getting references. Today, even asking "How's the family?" or "How old are your kids?" can get you into legal problems.

Second, everyone in America is trimming layers of middle management. This flattening of organizations is eliminating 35-60 percent of all middle management jobs. As a result, we have wider spans of control, needing to do our jobs with fewer people overall but having more people directly reporting to us than before.

The old rule of thumb for span of control was having five to seven people reporting to you. The new conventional wisdom is eleven to fifteen. We're quickly moving to the point where fifteen to twenty-five will not be unheard of or considered ineffective.

We have to do more work, better, faster, cheaper, and with fewer people. So the people we do have count more.

And in the process, the field of qualified candidates has grown.

Yes. The job market is filled with people looking for employment. In the early 1980s, it was hard to find really top-quality executives. Now, the question is, "How do I choose the best of the eighty qualified people who just sent in résumés?"

The screening process has become unbelievably cumbersome and complex. We are buried in raw data and résumés, and if we don't have a process to help in screening out quickly, we're dead. People provide tremendous amounts of conflicting, contradictory data—we need to be able to separate relevant information from the irrelevant.

What are some of the most common hiring mistakes?

One is going on "gut instinct"—intuition. I'm a strong believer in intuition, but if it's not balanced with a sound, logical thinking process, it's hard to tell whether your intuition is right or wrong. The tendency is to go with people we like, which may or may not correlate with their ability to do the job.

Another mistake is not defining the job first. We jump into the interview and hiring process before we know what we want the person to do. Without a job description, we can't accurately ask ourselves what qualities and qualifications a person would need. When we evaluate people with no formalized standard for evaluation, we're back to gut instinct.

Prejudices and biases are also a big factor in bad hiring decisions. Basically we have the "halo or horns effect"—generalizing a notable trait or accomplishment as representative of success in any endeavor. The dilemma is that we are people making decisions about people. But there's not much we can do about bias, except to be aware of it, push by it, and document our conclusions.

A related mistake is to assume that because a person is good in one field, he will naturally be good in another. For instance, being a good NFL linebacker doesn't mean a guy will be a good executive.

So that is the "halo effect." What does the "horns effect" look like?

Typical hiring managers engage in the process of disqualifying people, not qualifying them. They focus on weaknesses, hunt for them, and when they find them, disqualify the individual. This happens 90 percent of the time. Positive information gathered through an interview or from a reference typically carries much less weight than negative information.

Management expert Peter Drucker said that if you won't accept weakness in any areas, be prepared to accept mediocrity. We need to match strengths with the situation, because when there are great strengths, they are counterbalanced by strong weaknesses.

Drucker tells the story of how President Lincoln went through seven generals in the Civil War, until he came to Ulysses S. Grant, who drank, smoked cigars, and swore. He had only one strength, Lincoln said, but it was an important one—he was a good man in a fight.

What are the consequences of a poor hiring decision?

They're big. First of all, we need to remember indirect dollar cost invariably is greater than direct dollar cost. Managers spend most of their time trying to assist mediocre staff members. The worst consequence is hiring a person who is marginal, not totally unqualified. Terrible mistakes manifest themselves immediately and can be dealt with. Marginal employees, however, always demand more time and management, sapping your organization's vitality.

If you are able to recruit high caliber people, you can spend more of your time planning and leveraging the strengths of those people rather than helping the weak links just survive. One good employee has the productivity of three marginal ones. CEOs at the highest level of industry repeatedly say their number one priority is to get enough of the right people in the right positions.

Then there's the morale factor. When we hire incapable people, it decreases morale across the board because existing employees find that we have lowered the standards. People love being around great people, and it motivates them to greater achievement.

What are key elements or guidelines for making good hiring decisions?

First, know the job. Not knowing the job you are seeking to fill is equivalent to a general sending people to war without knowing the lay of the land.

Then develop a short list of selection criteria. I call them "what counts factors," which describe a person with a high probability of being able to do the job.

In the Bible, we see three methods of choosing people:

▲ *God chooses*—Moses at the burning bush, Gideon at the winepress, Saul in the road.

▲ *God sends a person to choose another person*—Samuel sent to Bethlehem to choose a new king.

▲ *God sends people to choose others, but doesn't give them the names.* Every time this is done in the Word of God, however, a list of selection criteria or success factors is provided. We see examples of this in Exodus 14, Acts 6, Titus 1, and 1 Timothy 3. The selection criteria define the kind of person who has potential to be successful in the job as you have defined it.

Interviewing, references, and evaluations need to be based on past performance. The best indicator of what people will do is what they have done. If I'm looking for an assistant, I want candidates to discuss situations they have handled similar to those they will face in the job I'm seeking to fill.

In your book, you describe four information sources employers have for evaluating job candidates: the résumé, interviews, references, and testing. How important is testing in the selection process?

Testing is a great tool—if used properly. But most of the time, it's not. In our firm, we recommend putting most of the energy into interviewing and checking references thoroughly. Most of the time, employers use testing as a panacea or safety net to cover themselves in the face of shoddy referencing and interviewing. They see it as a way to shortcut the hard work of good selection, but it's not.

You devote a chapter to the concept of "calling." Does a sense of calling fit for a Christian in a corporate setting?

It has that potential. God has the prerogative, power, and privilege to call any individual to any situation—spiritual or secular—but *particular,* specific calls are the exception rather than the rule. One thing that I would look for in any individual, as a Christian executive, would be an individual who has a sense of calling in a broader sense—willing to go anywhere God sends (if there are no specific instructions, to the most logical place). And willing to subordinate everything—money, gifts, skills—to God. I look for men and women who have a general sense of calling, a desire to be all that God wants them to be, rather than a specific calling to "Acme Metal Works."

In business circles today, we often use the word "team." How much should the idea of people working in teams—as opposed to individual initiative—factor into a hiring decision?

In a ministry setting, there is no place for rugged individualism. The Great Commission is better termed the Great *Co-Mission.* The same is true in the corporate community—team up or team out in the face of global competition. Clients look for the ability to team up with others, developing individual gifts and strengths within the context of a team in an organizational environment.

Past performance is the principle: evidence of ability to perform well in a team setting. One of the key qualities you always look for is a cooperative, unselfish spirit, which the Bible describes in Philippians 2:3–4. This is best checked out through references—seeing if the candidate is someone who has a history of cooperation.

What should come first—a clearly defined job, or a top-notch, talented person whom you would love to have in your organization?

The job, definitely! You can't create jobs to suit people in today's world. Everybody's a top-notch person, a "10," in the right job. But if you don't craft the job just right, they won't look so good. In these days of lean, mean staffing, filling our wants is a luxury we typically cannot afford. We need to first determine what jobs we must have performed, and then seek out the best people to perform them.

Tips for Successful Interviews

Carefully prepare. "The interview looks deceptively easy on the surface, since you are talking back and forth. But to get the information you need, questions must be carefully constructed in advance. For example, if you need to know how the job candidate will respond under stress, you need questions that focus on past behavior."

▲ Take effective notes. "If you don't, you won't remember who said what or what your impressions were at the time."

▲ Let the interviewee do the talking. "So often, the interviewer does more talking than the interviewee, and as a result leaves the interview without a lot of information."

▲ Build an atmosphere of rapport. "You have to help the candidate feel willing to take the risk of being transparent and honest. Ask yourself, 'If I were being interviewed, what would make me feel safe enough to be candid?' Then seek to create that atmosphere."

▲ Stay inside legal bounds. "A lot of people step over the legal line in interviewing. Today, we can't ask questions about age, family, national origin, religion, or financial affairs. In most states, however, it is legal to run a credit check."

Pat MacMillan points out, "The goal of our evaluation process is to gain insight into the relative qualifications of our candidates. An interview, in the ideal sense, is a time for asking a series of carefully crafted questions that allow us to capture this insight."

Chapter 41

Hiring: Art, Science, or Act of Faith?

Lessons on attracting key people

Curt Smith

What is hiring? To some, it is an art, relying on intuition, instinct, and the ability to read people. Others approach it primarily as a science, relying on personality tests, extensive interviews, and background checks. Still others generally engage in hiring as an act of faith, committing hiring decisions to prayer, asking God to bring the right people into the business.

No matter which of these basic patterns they favor, top executives agree that among their foremost responsibilities is finding the right person for the right position.

I interviewed three top executives, asking what lessons they have learned in attracting key people to their businesses. They agreed on several points, such as seeking qualified individuals who are proven performers and taking prudent measures such as checking references. But they also reflected different approaches to the problems and opportunities connected to the hiring process.

The Art of Reading People

John Keeble Sr., president and CEO of Investors Financial Group based in Atlanta, Georgia, has cultivated the art of "reading people." But he admits he does not "always get it right."

Given his other responsibilities and the size of his company—with fifty internal staff and about five hundred salespeople—Keeble participates only in hiring key executives. In filling those slots, he seeks proven performers who "are competent first, then I look for values second."

In his business, which offers personal financial planning and insurance services, Keeble also looks for "a person who is well aware of himself or herself." That person, he explained, is open, can communicate well, and has no "hidden agenda" that will interfere with the quality of communication and information flow necessary to operate the company.

This approach figured in a recent hiring decision, a top executive with his firm who will earn a six-figure salary before any bonuses are paid. The decision was relatively easy, Keeble says, because he was familiar with his past performance in the financial services industry. "He had an outstanding record with a big life insurance company, and he's an outstanding man."

Having conducted interviews for approximately one thousand general staff positions and fifty to seventy-five executives over the years, Keeble feels, "I can really read people now, but I don't get 'em right every time."

One example occurred several years ago in a previous company he owned.

"I hired one fellow for a management role. He had been an outside salesman. He was a good man," Keeble emphasized, "but when I put him in an operational role where he had to take some heat from people, things quickly fell apart.

"He would blow up and lose his temper. Within two months, we had to undo it (the hiring decision). He did take it well."

Arriving at a hiring decision does not end the process, Keeble says. He believes in remaining involved after a job is filled.

"I have a tendency, when I see yellow flags (problems), to talk about it," he points out. "I want bad news early if things are not going well." At the same time, he strives "to treat people with dignity and respect even when they mess up."

Boss Helps Set the Tone

When you want the best possible employees to make the best possible product, one of the ways to communicate this message is for the boss to be involved in hiring decisions. This is the view of Jim Blankemeyer, president and CEO of MetoKote Corporation of Lima, Ohio.

MetoKote, which employs 1,100 workers in fourteen plants in the Eastern United States, coats metal parts for the automotive and heavy equipment industries, as well as parts for computers and other specialized uses.

"In the last two years, I have reintroduced myself back into it," Blankemeyer says of his firm's hiring decisions. About five or six years ago, he "backed off," but later reversed that decision to stress the company's overall commitment to quality.

"We're taking a lot more time in our hiring," he points out, reflecting the more scientific approach. The hiring process at MetoKote now includes extensive interviewing, detailed background checks, and personality testing.

Blankemeyer is very involved in hiring the executive staff, but also participates in plant manager hirings "and a level or two below that." He sometimes meets with other potential employees just to shake their hands and spend a few minutes with them.

"We need the best. I think that's important," Blankemeyer emphasizes. "I set the tone" in pursuing that goal, thus requiring a formal and structured process at MetoKote.

Handle with Prayer

When Clayton Brown and two partners in 1974 began an investment banking firm in Chicago, specializing in municipal bonds, "our motivation and commitment was to be Christ's representative in the marketplace and to be faithful to His name."

This gave rise to a hiring process that Brown says "is not very scientific," but has served Clayton Brown & Associates, Inc. well in fulfilling its faith mission over the years, even as it expanded into a wider range of bond trading and financial planning services.

"We established a policy of not hiring only Christians," he states. "We looked for the best person for the job."

Given the firm's guiding motivation, Brown has always explained to potential employees the environment in which they would work. "We certainly don't have people who habitually use vulgarity or use the Lord's name in vain," he says. In addition to honoring God, this has created a professional climate on the trading desks that Brown believes has been good for business and assures clients of his firm's professionalism.

Today, Brown is chairman and CEO of the investment firm, which employs 175 people in six offices, including New York City and Chicago, the company's headquarters. He serves as the company's chief policy maker, having bought out his original partners. Prayer, he asserts, is central to his decision making.

"I frequently pray and ask God to guide us and bring the right people into the business," he says.

Brown attributes those prayers and the firm's guiding motivations as reasons for its success in attracting the right people. "We really have had very little trouble."

But prayer, he points out, is not an isolated factor in his success in personnel matters. The company does a thorough reference check and makes certain that key candidates interview with a member of his senior management team. Beyond that, "it's sort of a seat-of-the-pants thing."

Chapter 42

Selecting the Best

Five steps to reducing your hiring risks

Millard N. MacAdam

We understand the importance of godly men and women, driven by godly motivation, to accomplish God's work. But the principle is similar in the business world. Invest the time to recruit people of high character, competence, and commitment, or you put both your career and your company's future success at risk.

I have found that by following five proven steps you will significantly reduce hiring risks. These steps will help you select the best person from a field of candidates: both in terms of character and values that match those of your company, and in competence in terms of having a demonstrable history of doing well the tasks required in the specific job you are seeking to fill.

The first two steps are critical *before* you place your "Help Wanted" ad:

1. *Determine the specific character traits, attitudes, and values needed.* What attributes must a person demonstrate to function

within the unique "company culture" you want to develop and maintain? Define each and attach a list of observable behaviors that would reflect those character traits, attitudes, or values.

2. *Determine the specific performance tasks and competency standards required to get the job done well.* Describe these in behavioral terms that are observable.

3. *Determine the information to be uncovered during your interview.* Seek advice from people who have either successfully filled a similar position or have worked with people serving in the type of job you desire to fill. Their advice can help you determine the right questions to ask the candidates.

You want information that addresses specific character traits that will enable a person to become a committed, motivated contributor to the achievement of your company's vision, values, mission, and goals. You also need information about the candidate's technical competence—knowledge, understanding, and skills—needed to do a solid job.

4. *Design a basic list of interview questions that will serve as guidelines for each interview.* Question design has been a major weakness in many of the corporate interview and selection processes I have evaluated and helped to strengthen.

Business owners, executives, and managers tend to:

▲ Talk too much.

▲ Ask irrelevant questions.

▲ Fail to evaluate the "can do" and "will do" that candidates need to successfully do the job.

▲ Ask "What would you do?" types of theory questions. "Theory" questions let candidates off the hook—they don't have to provide information about performance that actually took place in doing their last job.

5. *Ask proactive interview questions.* This is how you find out if the candidate can actually "dribble the ball down court" in ten seconds and make two out of three shots from fifteen feet out. By design, proactive questions have a past action orientation.

They cause the candidates to tell what they did to successfully complete a quality job. For example, to learn how well a person could handle complaints over the phone, you could ask:

▲ "Over the last six months, about how many complaint calls did you handle?" (This tells frequency of experience.)

▲ "What are the specific things you did to handle your most difficult complaint call?" (This tells if they understand and are willing to apply interpersonal, problem-solving, and conflict-resolution skills.)

Once candidates start telling what they did rather than what they would do, they tend to continue doing so. They open up and offer a lot of valuable information about performance competencies, character, and commitment to achieve good results.

Keep asking action-oriented questions. Follow-up questions might be, "What are the most successful things you did regularly to make sure callers hang up happy and satisfied?" or "If I called some of the complainers you have handled, what would they say about the actions you took?"

Some candidates will avoid answering "proactive" interview questions in specific terms. When again and again they fail to clearly describe their previous actions on the job, cut the interview short and don't waste any more of your time. This is a strong signal that they lack confidence to do the job, haven't done the job before, don't know what to do on the job, or don't want to be held accountable for doing the job once they get hired.

Colossians 3:23 admonishes us, "Whatever you do, work at it with all your heart, as working for the Lord, not for men." This applies to every area of our lives, including the process of selecting the right people to enable our companies to provide the best possible products and services for our customers.

By following the steps I have outlined, you will improve the likelihood of selecting talented, motivated people who are committed to doing their jobs well and making your company look good. They also will save you the personal stress and time wasted by hiring and having to deal with a poor employee.

*We proclaim him, admonishing and
teaching everyone with all wisdom, so
that we may present everyone perfect in
Christ.*

—Colossians 1:28

It All Has to Start with Christ

*H*ave you ever tried to drive a car when it was out of gas? Or
have you attempted to watch TV when the set was unplugged?
It doesn't work, does it? Without the required fuel—the
power—the task is impossible. But this is exactly what some of
us seek to do in the workplace. We try to maintain consistent
lives of integrity, moral purity, love, mercy, compassion, wisdom,
and balance without being tied into the Power Source.

We focus on the world around us, instead of the God above.
We invest our lives pursuing the temporary, while neglecting the
eternal. We try to do for the Lord what only the Lord can
do—through us. We become so immersed in spiritual activity
that we never have time "to know Christ and the power of his
resurrection and the fellowship of sharing in his sufferings,
becoming like him in his death, and so, somehow, to attain to
the resurrection from the dead" (Phil. 3:10–11).

There certainly is nothing wrong with lofty motives, good
intentions, and high standards of behavior. However, if the

225

things we do are to have any lasting significance, they must be done in partnership with Christ. As Jesus said in John 15:5, "apart from me you can do nothing (NASB)." It is equally true, as the apostle Paul declared, "I can do everything through him who gives me strength" (Phil. 4:13).

In this final section, we look at the vital issue of being rightly related to Christ, not only by being assured of receiving Him as Savior, but also by daily practicing His lordship in our lives. Consider in these concluding articles what it really means to be a follower of Christ.

Chapter 43

Being Ready Always

Divine appointments can come unexpectedly

Phil Downer

A challenging directive in the Bible for people in business today, I believe, is found in Colossians 4:5, "Be wise in the way you act toward outsiders; make the most of every opportunity." The problem with this passage is that it does not include words like "when it is convenient to do so" or "if you feel up to it" or "when it fits your schedule." It does, however, say *"every opportunity."* As an attorney, I can assure you, there is no exclusion clause in this passage.

An Old Friend

God often brings opportunities at seemingly inopportune times. I don't think He will ever let me forget one such occasion several years ago while I was still in private law practice. I was returning home on a Friday evening from Washington National Airport, on one of those flights where they just pack you in, cattle car style. The week had been filled with depositions, courtroom appearances, the almost continual clamor of legal conflict.

As I found my seat on the plane, I slumped down and went to sleep almost immediately, hardly noticing the man seated next to me. All I wanted was to be left alone so I could unwind.

The thud of the jet's wheels on the runway in Atlanta jolted me out of slumber. It occurred to me that I still had not paid any attention to the man beside me, but inwardly I shrugged, "Too late, we're getting off the plane now." As I reached under the seat in front of me to pull out my litigation case, my "neighbor" noticed the name tag.

"Phil Downer!" he said. I turned to see it was my big brother from our fraternity days at Southern Methodist University. My old buddy, yet during a ninety-five-minute flight from Washington, D.C., to Atlanta, I had not said one word to him! And now we were leaving the plane, and he was eager to get home.

A missed opportunity! I had slept through God's appointment for my old friend and me that day. I regretted not being able to tell how I had almost lost everything close to me, including my marriage, until some businessmen reached out to me and helped introduce me to Jesus Christ.

No Second Chances

Although he was rushed, we exchanged a few pleasantries and promised to get together, since he is regional manager in Atlanta for a national corporation. I have called him several times and talked about old times and our lives now, but the conversations are always brief. He also has declined my invitations to Christian Business Men's Committee outreach meetings.

I would like to say that I learned my lesson that day and have been diligent to "make the most of every opportunity," but it seems I'm a slow learner. Last spring, on a plane bound for Denver, en route to our CBMC staff conference in Colorado Springs, my wife, Susy, and I were trying to get caught up on our homework for the personal financial management Bible study we were attending.

So intent was I on the week's assignment, I hardly noticed the boy seated next to me. At least he wasn't a businessman, right? About halfway from Atlanta to Denver, I thought it might be a good idea to chat with the young fellow, who was about twelve years old. I wondered if he knew the Lord. Judging from the title of the book he was reading, it seemed likely that he did not.

We struck up a conversation. As I asked a few simple questions about his life, I learned that his mother had divorced his father after getting involved with another man she met at a business conference. She and the other man had since married and were sitting about ten rows behind us.

The boy spoke frankly about his hurts. I told him that because of circumstances in my own childhood, I could identify with some of his struggles.

As we talked, I explained how God enabled me to overcome this pain by asking Jesus Christ to come into my life. He seemed genuinely interested, so I pulled a copy of "Steps to Peace with God" from my pocket and asked if I could read it to him. He agreed. I showed him that we all are born separated from God by sin, with only one way to bridge this separation—Jesus Christ.

We looked at the illustration of a chasm showing a holy God on one side and man separated from Him by sin on the other. "Are you on this side, with God, or on man's side?" I asked. "I'm on man's side," the boy answered, "but I would like to be on God's side."

How thrilling it was as he bowed his head with me to ask the Lord Jesus into his life. He was sitting in an aisle seat, with people walking back and forth, and his mother and new stepfather rows behind us, but that made no difference to him. Out loud, this youngster called out to God, making the most important decision of his life.

A Continous Commission

How thankful I was for pausing from my Bible study homework to talk with him. As we read in 1 Peter 3:15 (KJV), we need to be "ready *always* to give an answer" [author's emphasis] or as the *New American Standard Bible* translates it in legal terms, "to make a defense . . . for the hope that is in you."

I confess I'm still not always sensitive to the needs of people around me, although my goal is to fully allow Christ to live through me. Like most people, I get preoccupied with other concerns, but I'm learning. We never know when God has arranged a divine appointment for us, whether on an airplane, in a restaurant, in the office, or in our neighborhoods. May the Lord enable us to "make the most of *every* opportunity" for His glory by focusing on Him and letting Him work through us in all things.

Chapter 44

I Could Have Been There!

How the world trade center bombing hit close to home

Jerry Molnar

At 12:18 P.M. on February 26, 1993, a huge explosion rocked the World Trade Center complex in New York City. Five persons died; more than one thousand people were injured. The terrorist bomb blast occurred on the B2 underground level of the Vista International Hotel's public parking garage. It left a crater 200 feet wide and several stories deep.

I remember that day well. In fact, the B2 level is usually where I park my car after commuting from my home in Bayonne, New Jersey. For the past ten years, I have maintained an office for my personnel agency on the 107th floor of One World Trade Center.

As my wife, Camy, watched the newscasts of the terrible aftermath of the explosion, I couldn't help but think, *There but for the grace of God go I.*

Our original plan was to drive into the city, work until about noon, then leave for a Christian Business Men's Committee couples retreat in Carlisle, Pennsylvania. But Camy was ill that morning, so I canceled our reservations and stayed home with her.

Had we followed our plan, I might have been in the garage when the explosion occurred. It was an eerie feeling, watching emergency personnel search through the rubble, thinking I could have been among the dead, or one of the casualties.

I Was "Lucky"

Some of my friends said I was "lucky." I'll tell you why I don't think that word applies.

At one time, "luck" was prominent in my vocabulary. From age sixteen, when I got my first job on Wall Street delivering securities for a brokerage firm, I considered myself lucky. As I became more closely involved in commodities and securities investing, good luck seemed my way of life.

By 1965, I was running part of a brokerage firm in St. Louis, at the time the eleventh largest in the world. From there I moved into the personnel business, becoming a well-paid "headhunter" for the securities industry.

From 1978 to 1983, I was a 50 percent partner in three lucrative personnel agencies. My "secret" to success was hiring people with addictions. Since they needed a lot of money to feed their costly habits, I felt they would work harder—and they did.

Aquiring Addictions

At the same time, I was acquiring addictions of my own: alcohol and gambling. I traded heavily in commodities, which gave me the biggest high in the world. Some days I could make fifteen thousand dollars before I got out of bed, simply with a phone call to the London market. I could make, and lose, phenomenal amounts of money in minutes. After a while, it became simply a numbers game, wanting to accumulate higher and higher numbers.

The only time I heard the word *God* was at the gambling tables in Atlantic City, New Jersey—never spoken in a reverent way. I really didn't know if there was a God or not, but just in case, I would try making deals with Him. If my luck turned bad, I would think something like, *God, if you let me hit this next number, I'll give you half of the profits.* (By the time I got back home, God had taken a major pay cut.)

I did some things that I'm not proud of today, but they show the kind of person I was. Once Camy bought me a race horse. I actually tried to fix the horse's first race. I went into the jockeys' locker room and boldly announced, "I'm Jerry Molnar, my horse is Marseilles, and we can all make some money if you'll listen to me." Those jockeys scattered like they had just seen a ghost.

In a Tunnel

Alcohol also had a strong hold on me. Often I left work in the evening having already consumed several drinks. One night, during the five o'clock rush hour, I was so drunk that I stopped my car *in* the Holland Tunnel—which goes under the Hudson River to connect New York City and New Jersey—and walked away. Then I called Camy to come and get me.

You can imagine the traffic jam that created. The next day, the number one topic of conversation was "some guy" who parked his car in the Holland Tunnel. I couldn't believe that *I* was the guy.

Not long after that I realized something had to be done about my drinking problem. I joined Alcoholics Anonymous. This proved to be a turning point for me in more ways than one.

May 5, 1983, was the worst day of my life. As I drove to work that morning, I was celebrating three months of abstaining from alcohol. A friend I had met at AA, Sean, had been a big help to me through this time.

Breach of Contract

At the office, my partner was waiting for me with his lawyer. They served legal documents stating I was no longer a partner in the three agencies. I was being terminated due to breach of contract. What this really meant was that during my weeks of sobriety, trying to get my life together, my sales had dropped substantially.

My partner was the administrator, while I was the builder of the company, responsible for bringing in new business. He said I had failed to fulfill my role as a partner. He also didn't like the idea that I had become the only one in the place who didn't drink or use drugs.

Instantly my life, which had revolved around my career, turned upside down. One of the first things I did was call Sean, saying I needed to see him right away. We agreed to meet at a donut shop in Hoboken, New Jersey. When he heard I had been thrown out of my own company, Sean responded, "Praise God! This is great news." How could this be great news?

Sean invited Camy and me over for dinner that evening and I accepted. He was all I had to lean on at the time, and the hours in between were nerve-wracking.

The Real Problem

After dinner, Sean explained that losing my agencies wasn't my biggest problem. The real problem, he said, was sin—rebellion against God and failure to live up to His perfect standards. "For all have sinned and fall short of the glory of God," he quoted from the Bible.

To solve the problem of sin, he said, God had come to earth in the form of a man—Jesus Christ. Jesus not only provided great moral teaching, but more important, suffered a terrible death on a cross to serve as the payment—once and for all—for our sins.

This payment, however, offered as a gift, must be received, Sean said. He recited another Bible verse, "but as many as received Him (Jesus Christ), to them He gave the right to become children of God" (John 1:12, NASB). The alternative? Eternal separation from God.

Did We Want the Gift?

Jesus Christ was the way to find real peace in life, my friend assured us, and I knew I didn't have much of that. The question was, were we willing to receive the gift of eternal life that God was offering?

As Sean talked, I was reminded of a business client, Tom Vitale. I had placed Tom in several positions, and he had told me similar things for over six years. He had even told me that the Bible says it is easier for a camel to get through the eye of a needle than for a rich man to enter the kingdom of heaven.

Frankly, as Sean kept telling us about God and the Bible, my immediate reaction was that he was a nut. But I knew he really cared about me, so I continued to listen.

When Camy and I had arrived at Sean's home, the thought of praying to invite Jesus Christ into our lives had never entered our minds. But our pain was so severe, at Sean's urging, that is what we did. He assured us God would help us, even with a lawsuit I was considering against my former partner. As we drove home, I remember thinking, *I don't know what good that little rinky-dink prayer will do.*

A New Direction

The next morning I started to find out. Setting out to find new office space to start a new agency, I discovered a perfect location in the World Trade Center. This kind of space is very desirable as a status symbol, but the real estate manager had never let personnel agencies in before. This time he let me rent an office.

I was literally starting over. I had just received an income tax refund check—for the exact amount needed for the office space. My supplies consisted of a stack of napkins, a pen, and a telephone.

From Worst to the Best

God also "helped" me with the lawsuit—He showed me it wasn't necessary. My attorney felt certain I could win my case, but after a few months of experiencing peace in my life for the first time, I was relieved just to be out of the business. Instead of being the worst day of my life, May 5, 1983, had turned out to be the best.

A couple of years later, I was introduced to the Christian Business Men's Committee. The impact of this ministry on Camy and me has been incredible. We have met other Christians in business, and our lives have been tremendously enriched spiritually. One man, Dick Arthur, took me under his wing and showed great patience in dealing with my many questions. He has become one of my best friends.

Not for Profit

Some people believe in "prosperity theology," that God wants to make all of His children rich. In a spiritual sense this is true, but materially I have found much the opposite. While I have been able to earn a living, I made a lot more money before I committed my life to Christ.

In fact, I have turned down a number of promising business deals because they would have required forming partnerships with non-Christians. The Bible teaches that we should not become "unequally yoked" with non-believers. I have seen some of the deals prove as financially rewarding as expected, so I have wondered at times if I did the right thing. But I have learned God doesn't make mistakes; His principles remain as true today as they were two thousand years ago.

My goal is to remain faithful and obedient to Him, relying on His promise to provide for all my needs "according to His riches in glory in Christ Jesus" (Phil. 4:19, NASB).

So when I heard about the World Trade Center explosion and realized I could have been there, I never considered it luck that I stayed home. It was because of a loving God who, in the final years of the twentieth century, still works "all things together for good to those who love Him, to those who are called according to His purpose" (Rom. 8:28, NKJV).

Chapter 45

Leaving the Right Impression

Character leaves its own mark on the people we meet

Steven Farrar

About one hundred years ago, G. K. Chesterton made a shrewd observation: "The great science of fingerprints . . . has produced its principal or ultimate effect on the world, which is this: That whereas a gentleman was expected to put on gloves to dance with a lady, he may now be expected to put on gloves in order to strangle her. These changes in etiquette, or fine shades of fashion, may or may not correspond with an improvement in dancing or a decrease in strangling."

Before the advent of fingerprinting, a criminal didn't need to worry about gloves since fingerprints were not a factor. Fingerprints are a telltale sign that a particular individual has been in a particular place, even if they deny it, and deny it even with overzealous contradictions and preposterous theatrics to impress a jury. Fingerprints don't lie.

A person's character doesn't leave fingerprints. But it does make impressions. Impressions are the fingerprints of character.

Fingerprints are found on desks, mirrors, and doorknobs. But what about the fingerprints of character? Where do you find them?

The fingerprints of character are found in personal relationships. Character leaves its mark, its lasting impressions, on the lives of the people that we interact with daily.

Sometimes the impressions are negative. When I was in college, I was privileged to sit under the teaching of a nationally known Christian author. This man had a large sphere of influence, and I was very fortunate to have access to such a gifted teacher. Several of my friends also were involved in his ministry. We were thrilled to have entry to someone who made such an impact on so many people.

Years later, if you were to ask me or my friends, they would tell you that this particular individual made an astonishingly strong first impression. But they would also tell you that as time went by, it became apparent that here was a man whose life was characterized by lies and deceit.

This guy was strong on first impressions, but as the impressions got into the tens, the hundreds, and the thousands, his true character became increasingly clear. One of my friends is convinced that the man is a pathological liar. But it took years of negative impressions for him to believe that. Quite frankly, the man's reputation preceded him, and his reputation was so strong that we expected his character to match it. It didn't.

We were devastated, but we weren't the only ones—so were his wife and his children when they discovered he had been lying for years to cover his adultery. They, too, thought he was a man of character. But he wasn't. He was simply a man of reputation, with a trail of broken relationships left behind him to mark his "ministry" and his family.

Rare and Noteworthy

Every significant relationship in your life has your fingerprints all over it—the fingerprints of your character. And those impressions on another person's life are true indications of what your character is really like.

We are living in a secular society. Our particular society has legislated Jesus Christ out of the classroom, the university, the media, and just about everything else. How in the world is a secular person ever going to come across the reality of Jesus Christ?

I suggest that the key may be an encounter with your personal character—not your personality, not your success, not your net worth, not your education, but your character. For in a secular society where reputation and appearance are valued over character, a person with genuine character is a rare and noteworthy exception.

Godly character in a secular society stands out. It makes an impression; it leaves fingerprints. And a close examination of those fingerprints always leads to the same Person. If Jesus Christ has gripped your life, then His fingerprints will be all over you. His fingerprints will be on your money, your expense account, your tax return, your marriage, your kids, your speech, and all your other relationships.

Why is it so important that His fingerprints be all over your character? Because for some people, the existence of those fingerprints is the only tangible proof they will ever see of the reality of Jesus Christ. Here's the bottom line: As He imprints your character, so your character will imprint others.

Chapter 46

A Crash Course in Faith

A lesson in strength and weakness

Kennard Barackman

One of the unsettling aspects of change is that sometimes it just happens, without notice, whether you are ready for it or not. I discovered that one morning while making my usual drive to work at AT&T in Pittsburgh.

Traveling on Route 30 at 6:50 A.M., I was enjoying the start of a beautiful, sunny day. It was March 27, 1990, and as my 1981 Volkswagen Rabbit smoothly kept pace with the morning traffic, I remember thinking how well the car was running. The engine had just been rebuilt a few months before, and I planned to keep the Rabbit another four years until my two sons finished college.

As I approached an intersection, I saw that my signal was green. Glancing at the speedometer, which indicated fifty miles per hour, the speed limit, I continued into the intersection.

Suddenly something flashed into my field of vision from my driver's side window. I quickly turned my head and looked directly into the eyes of a twenty-two-year-old woman a split second before the car she was driving collided with mine. She had failed to notice that her light was red until it was too late to stop.

Point of Impact

Her vehicle struck the left side of mine, ramming it into the slower traffic lane and then into a guard rail. My car finally skidded to a stop in the middle of Route 30.

I'm a strong believer in seat belts, but I was not wearing one that morning because it was broken and I hadn't found time to have it repaired. That saved my life.

When the other car struck mine, it pushed into the driver's seat. I was thrown to the other side of my car. If my seatbelt had been on, I would have been crushed. As it was, my body hit the passenger door so hard it made a dent from the inside out.

I was knocked out for a couple of minutes, and when I regained consciousness, a man was trying to open my car door and help me get out. At the same time, he was holding a handkerchief above my eyebrow to stop the bleeding from a deep gash I had suffered.

My left leg had become wedged between the clutch and brake pedal, and my body was turned toward the back of the car, so I had to work myself free. The pain was so excruciating I'm amazed that I didn't go into shock.

My only thought was to pray, *Lord Jesus, please be with me and help me with this pain!* I had committed my life to Christ four years earlier, but had never sensed such an urgent need for Him. As I prayed, an incredible sense of peace swept over me, briefly blotting out the pain. I didn't hear an audible voice, but sensed God telling me, "What you believe in Me and in Jesus Christ is 100 percent true." I had already believed that, but those words gave me great assurance that He would remain by me through this ordeal. I also knew that whatever happened, my eternal relationship with Him was secure.

Soon emergency technicians arrived. The woman driving the other car had suffered only minor injuries, so I received most of their attention.

They took me to Westmoreland Hospital in Greensburg, where physicians determined my left thigh bone had been fractured in four places, and my left ankle was broken, along with all the ribs on my left side. One lung had collapsed and my spleen had to be removed. During surgery a nerve that affects the vocal chords was bruised, causing me to temporarily lose my voice.

After the initial surgery, I was transported to Presbyterian University Hospital in Pittsburgh because the doctors suspected I had suffered heart damage. The upper aorta from my heart had been 90 percent detached, the surgeons discovered. Miraculously, a piece of fatty tissue had become wrapped around the aorta, sealing it enough to keep blood flowing through me until the damage could be detected.

In all, I was in surgery for seventeen and a half hours. When they finally wheeled me out of the operating room, my chest and upper abdomen looked like I had a zipper, and a metal plate had been attached with screws and wires from my left knee to the hip joint.

Most of that time, my wife, Carol, sat anxiously and prayerfully in the hospital waiting rooms. She had been called at work about 7:30 A.M. Because she was so nervous, a friend took her to the hospital in Greensburg. On the way, they had to pass through the intersection on Route 30 and saw my demolished car. Despite the appearance of the car, Carol clung to hope that my injuries were minor.

At the hospital, however, she was informed of the extent of my injuries, that I was undergoing extensive surgery, and plans were being made to transport me by Life Flight to Presbyterian University Hospital in Pittsburgh. After calling our two sons, Chris and Tim, Carol then called a friend in Latrobe and a Christian Business Men's Committee friend in Pittsburgh, asking them to start a prayer chain for me. Weeks later, we learned that people in many states had been praying for us.

Surrounded by Friends

Tim and Carol then drove to the Pittsburgh hospital, where they met Chris, who was a student at the University of Duquesne. Within minutes, friends began arriving to offer emotional and prayer support for my family in the trauma waiting room.

One CBMC friend, Sam Ware, loaned Carol his Bible to read while she was waiting to receive word from the surgeons. She didn't let go of it for seventeen days!

A hospital chaplain also came in and minutes later commented that he had expected to find a group of emotionally distraught people but, instead, found himself being ministered to and encouraged.

After the surgeons finally finished working on me, they ordered a CAT scan to make sure that I had not suffered any brain damage. Thankfully, the test results were negative.

My Wife's Reactions

Eighteen hours after she had first learned of my accident, Carol and our sons were allowed into the trauma unit to see me. I will let her tell you her reactions:

"Ken had every tube you could think of coming out of him, he was on a breathing machine, and his left side was humongous, swollen three times its normal size.

"Amazingly, I didn't panic but thought confidently that God would use this situation for good. I felt no anger toward anyone—God or the woman whose car struck Ken's. Actually, I'm a wimp, not a strong person at all, but the Lord gave His strength to help me through that time. The thought that Ken could die never entered my mind, even though the doctors had told me that the first twenty-four to forty-eight hours were the most critical, that he could suffer a stroke or heart attack.

"Looking at his left side, I thought, 'This is what Satan has done,' and looking at Ken's undamaged right side, I could see God's handiwork.

"Ken was only in the trauma unit for seven days, and each time we went to see him, we could see how the Lord was bringing healing, changing him for the better."

Overall, I was in three hospitals for a total of seventeen days. Before the accident, I had stated that I wanted to lose forty pounds and had asked God to help me get my weight under control. During my hospitalization and the recuperation period, I lost forty pounds.

Today, I am still recovering from some of the effects of the accident. Some pain remains in my left leg and hip, especially when I do a lot of walking. There is also general soreness and some numbness. But what stays with me the most are the lessons that we have learned as a result.

One is God's incredible provision. The defective seat belt, I know, was not a coincidence. The fatty tissue that somehow wrapped itself around my damaged aorta, the surgeon told me after I was moved from the trauma unit, was "a miracle of God." And we will never forget our many Christian friends who surrounded us with love, support, and prayers.

About a week after my accident, I had to undergo a long series of X-rays to determine if there had been any other undetected injuries and to see how well I was healing. At one point, even though it still hurt too much even to touch, I had to lie on my left side in the X-ray tube.

The pain I felt was so intense, the minutes spent on my side seemed like hours. "God, why did you save my life just to let me suffer like this?" I prayed. Immediately, the thought came to me, *What are you complaining about? The Lord Jesus died for your sins, and His pain was a thousand times more than you will ever know.*

Within twenty minutes, I was back in my room. As the medication quickly relieved my distress, I thought about the agony that Jesus endured for me, hanging for hours on a rough, wooden cross. More than ever before, I realized that my life truly is not my own, that I have been bought with a price.

Looking back, Carol and I both see 1990 as the best year of our lives, because the Lord has taught us these things we probably could not have learned any other way.

Desires Realized

Before the accident, we had attended a CBMC leaders' conference and marveled at some of the testimonies about what God had done in people's lives. Carol had commented on how great it would be for us to be able to do that one day, admitting that she was too shy to stand up and talk before a group of people. Again, the Lord gives us the desires of our hearts in unusual ways.

At the hospital, we both had many opportunities to talk with family members, friends, visitors, and the hospital staff about Jesus Christ. We have also been asked on a number of occasions to speak publicly about our "adventure." God has even taken care of Carol's anxiety. She said before the emcee introduced us she was shaking, but as soon as we stood up to speak that first time, the Lord took over and her nervousness disappeared.

I suppose most of all, I have a greater understanding of what the apostle Paul meant when he wrote, "for to me to live is Christ, and to die is gain" (Phil. 1:21, KJV). God has given me a deeper appreciation for what He has done for me and now, for the rest of my life, I'm determined to help others learn about Him, too.

Chapter 47

Taking Advantage of Change

Pointing others to Jesus

Phil Downer

The one quality that best seems to characterize our culture today is change, massive change on global, national, and personal levels.

We are quickly becoming a borderless world community so expansive and pervasive that we all personally feel the impact of world events, trends, and opinions on a daily basis. Technological advances now permit instantaneous interchange of information.

Shifting demographics, like the graying of America and the fragmentation of the family, are changing not only *what* America is, but also *who* America is. The ever-strengthening grip of secularism and a pluralistic society is placing greater value on choice than truth. A byproduct is the lowest level of commitment in our nation's history to institutions, relationships, and obligations.

I saw an example of this while my wife, Susy, and I were flying to Washington, D.C., to take part in a CBMC "ministry night."

The businessman next to me on the plane was headed to the nation's capital for some company meetings.

After the usual small talk, he asked about my travels. I explained we were going to speak at a couples' banquet. During the conversation, I wove in some comments about our broken marriage and told him how some godly men and women reached out to us for Christ and helped us to rebuild our relationship.

The Name of the Game

As we kidded about the difficulties of human relationships, I commented, "I assume your marriage is perfect, never involves arguments, disagreements, or strife, and you and your wife always think precisely the same on every topic." He chuckled, but then his face became serious as he responded, "Which marriage?" He had been married three times; his third marriage was in trouble and they were living apart.

The reason for their separation? She wanted to live in the city, while he preferred to live in the country!

Such a rationale for discarding a marriage might seem ludicrous, but this is where many people are today. Americans are making decisions that will shape the rest of their lives with less thought and reflection than they use for selecting a meal at a local restaurant.

In addition, the security we once felt as business and professional men has been dashed, replaced by great uncertainty and for some people, great apprehension. Between 1985 and 1990, 143 of the Fortune 500 companies disappeared from the list. It seems no one's job is safe anymore, whether you are CEO of General Motors or owner of a tiny "mom and pop" business.

All around us are people with tremendous needs and deep hurts. We can point them to the answer, which is Jesus Christ. But we can't wait for them to approach us; we must pursue them. Jesus did not instruct us to "wait for them to come"; He said, "*Go* therefore and make disciples of all the nations" (Matt. 28:19, NASB, emphasis added).

The Pursuit

In the Christian Business Men's Committee of USA, our mission is not to establish and carry out programs, but to pursue the people for whom Christ died, communicating the gospel through our lives, as well as through our words.

Although change is often difficult for us, change really is to our advantage—from a perspective of God's kingdom—since it underscores the uncertainties of the world in which we live. Someone, commenting on the rate and impact of change upon our culture, said "the lapse time between surprises is getting shorter." We, too, may be caught off guard by change, but our trust remains in an unchangeable, sovereign God.

Perhaps as we ourselves have struggled to deal with changes in our workplaces, our communities, and our homes, we can offer support and consolation to others. As we read in 2 Corinthians 1:4, He "comforts us in all our troubles, so that we can comfort those in any trouble with the comfort we ourselves have received from God."

One for All

As Christians, our faith offers the one true constant—God and His Word. The Lord tells us to be prepared for change. In 1 Chronicles 12:32, we are told of the "men of Issachar, who understood the times and knew what Israel should do." We, too, need to become wise observers of our times and understand how changes around us are affecting those whom we desire to reach with the good news of Christ.

The Bible also tells us not to tremble in the face of inevitable change. "Forget the former things; do not dwell on the past. See, I am doing a new thing! Now it springs up; do you not perceive it?" (Isa. 43:18–19).

Our task in CBMC—and as Christians in the American business world—is to discern what "new thing" God is doing and respond appropriately. As we read in Colossians 4:5–6, "Be wise in the way you act toward outsiders; make the most of every opportunity. Let your conversation be always full of grace, seasoned with salt, so that you may know how to answer everyone."

Our mission is to reach out, in many different ways, to people around us. Most business and professional men and women carry a deep sense of loneliness; they desperately need a friend who is genuine and sincere. We can be that friend. Make a commitment today: Make a friend, be a friend, lead that friend to an eternal relationship with Jesus Christ, and then, if possible, help that friend make the first unsteady but crucial steps toward spiritual maturity.

Afterword

At a missions conference, a visiting missionary greeted a member of the church. After exchanging the accustomed pleasantries, the missionary asked the young woman, "And what kind of work do you do?"

As a wide smile crept across her face, she replied, "I'm a disciple of Christ, cleverly disguised as a secretary."

What a wonderful perspective, don't you think? She didn't see her church involvement as something she did for God, and her job as something she did for herself. She didn't sense a fracture between her spiritual calling and her vocational calling. We each could make a similar declaration: "I'm a disciple of Christ, cleverly disguised as _____." *(You fill in the blank.)*

For more than fourteen years, serving on the staff of the Christian Business Men's Committee of USA, I have been in what I would term "vocational Christian work," but don't be misled. We are *all* in "full-time Christian service." After all, there is no such thing as a part-time Christian, and we are all called to serve the Lord. The only difference, as someone said, is where your paycheck comes from.

In the days before I came to know Christ, my impression of Christian businessmen, frankly, was not a good one. Christian businessman? *That,* I felt, was an oxymoron! Thankfully, I have since learned that is not really the case—although I still occasionally meet brothers and sisters who seem set on perpetuating the stereotype. They have "let the world squeeze them into its mold" as J. B. Phillips paraphrases Romans 12:2. They wrongly assume that while their faith works well on Sundays, it is best left behind on the weekdays.

How important is it for you and me to commit to representing the Lord, through our work and through our words? Every day, we labor alongside men and women who are drowning spiritually and desperately need someone brave enough to risk throwing them a life preserver. It is the evidence of our lives that convinces them that our life preserver is worth hanging onto. As Francis of Assisi once said, "Preach the Gospel all the time. When necessary, use words." But even if no one responds to our communications of Christ—at least that we recognize—our dedicated, diligent commitment to our work is an act of worship. "For we are to God the aroma of Christ among those who are being saved and those who are perishing" (2 Cor. 2:15).

As business and professional people, we live and work in a strategic segment of society. All around us we see evidence of a world gone, to use a fitting Spanish word, *loco.* "Where there is ignorance of God, crime runs wild," as Proverbs 29:18 is expressed so powerfully in *The Living Bible.* You and I can be used by God to dispel that ignorance among a mass of people who wield much of the influence and control much of the affluence of our nation—and the world. And it is from the business community that our present and future leaders come. We can play a part in restoring the traditional, God-centered values upon which the United States was founded—but seems to have forgotten.

What Is CBMC?

The Christian Business Men's Committee is a network of ministry teams committed to the critical process of evangelism and discipleship. Across the United States—and around the world—more than fifty thousand men and women are involved with CBMC. Their goal is to take the good news of Jesus Christ to one of the most critical and strategic segments of society, the business and professional world.

CBMC was founded in 1930, and has become an effective part of a growing movement dedicated to presenting Jesus Christ as Savior and Lord to business and professional men, and to develop Christian business and professional men to carry out the Great Commission. CBMC ministries are reaching out in marketplace settings in over fifty countries, with over six hundred fifty ministry teams and more than fifteen thousand members in the United States alone.

As women have gained prominence in the business community, many have benefited from participation in CBMC-sponsored endeavors, ranging from mealtime outreach meetings to small-group Bible discussions to personal discipling.

Suited for Both Office and Home

CBMC is a ministry that sees the workplace and the neighborhood as equally important settings for reaching out to business people for Jesus Christ. The business environment continues to be a place for demonstrating to employees, coworkers, and employees that "Jesus *does* work here." Some of the alternatives available through CBMC for this purpose are:

▲ Weekly meetings where Christian business and professional men meet for encouragement, Bible study, and prayer.

▲ Evangelistic outreach meetings, held at breakfast, lunch, or dinner, where prominent Christians in business tell their personal testimonies of how Jesus Christ touched their lives and urge uncommitted guests attending to consider the claims of Christ for themselves.

▲ "Business by the Book" seminars and Forums, at which business owners, CEOs, and top executives can study and discuss in depth what it means to run a business God's way.

▲ Capital Groups, at which young business leaders meet for motivation and encouragement in standing firm for Christ on the job.

With the home increasingly being a focal point for business as well as family life, many CBMC ministry activities are taking place in the neighborhood as well. Some of these include:

▲ The "Living Proof" small group video training series on relationship evangelism and personal discipleship.

▲ Small group evangelistic Bible studies of the Gospel of John.

▲ Crown Ministries studies on biblical perspectives about personal finances and stewardship.

▲ "Dad, the Family Shepherd" seminars for men and four-week "encouragement team" meetings.

▲ Men's accountability groups.

▲ Recreational outings where Christians and uncommitted friends can meet on "neutral ground" for fun, relaxation, and an opportunity to discuss issues of eternal importance.

▲ Home Bible studies and prayer groups for women.

A Ministry of Vision

In 1993 CBMC adopted the following vision statement:

"Compelled by Christ's love and empowered by God's Spirit, impacting the world by saturating the Business and Professional Community with the Gospel of Jesus Christ by establishing, equipping, and mobilizing teams where we work and live that yield spiritual reproducers."

God has not entrusted the mission of reaching the business and professional world to CBMC alone. But through the faithful use of many innovative, life-changing ministry tools and resources God has given, as well as through strategic alliances— with other marketplace ministries, denominations, and local churches—the men and women of CBMC are making a difference.

If you would like to learn more about CBMC, or become involved with a CBMC group in your area, write or call:

CBMC of USA
P.O. Box 3308
Chattanooga, TN 37404
1-800-566-CBMC

This Magazine Is for You!

If you have benefited from reading *Jesus Works Here*, you will enjoy *CONTACT Quarterly*, the quarterly magazine of the Christian Business Men's Committee of USA.

Many of the chapters which have been included in *Jesus Works Here* originally appeared in *CONTACT Quarterly*, which is dedicated to helping Christians in business learn how to relate their faith to the modern workplace in practical and effective ways.

If you would like to receive a complimentary copy of *CONTACT Quarterly* and information on how to subscribe, write to:

Subscription Secretary
CONTACT Quarterly
P.O. Box 3308
Chattanooga, TN 37404

Here's Additional Good Reading:

A companion book to *Jesus Works Here* is available. *The Complete Christian Businessman*, also edited by Robert J. Tamasy, covers important issues confronting business and professional people today. Topics include: the purpose of work, business ethics, leadership, partnerships, coping with failure, retirement, stress, personal accountability, entanglement, being an effective husband and father, sexual temptation, chemical dependency, personal money management, and debt.

Copies of *The Complete Christian Businessman* can be purchased from the CBMC of USA and retail for $15.00 plus shipping. To order *The Complete Christian Businessman*, write or call:

CBMC Materials Department
P.O. Box 3308
Chattanooga, TN 37404
1-800-566-CBMC

About the Authors

Joel Barker is president of Infinity, Ltd., in St Paul, Minnesota, an internationally known consulting firm that has pioneered the concept of strategic exploration. His latest book is *Paradigms: The Business of Discovering the Future.*

Kennard Barackman and his wife, Carol, live in Latrobe, Pennsylvania. Ken is a data networking account executive for AT&T. Carol is director of purchasing for GBC Materials Corp. They have two sons, Christopher and Timothy, and are raising their nephew, Eric. Ken is a chairman for CBMC in Pittsburgh.

Daniel M. Baker III is a senior systems engineer for United Sciences, Inc., in Gibsonia, Pennsylvania. He and his wife, Patti, have three children, Dana, Byron, and Amy, and reside in Pittsburgh. Dan is a CBMC member in Pittsburgh.

John C. Bird, Jr., is a regional sales executive with Chrysler Motor Company in Cincinnati, Ohio. He and his wife, Carole, have two sons, Daniel and John, and reside in West Chester, Ohio. John is a member of CBMC in the Cincinnati area.

Kenneth Blanchard is chairman of Blanchard Training and Development, Inc., in Escondido, California, which conducts training seminars, produces training materials, and consults with companies nationwide. He is the author of the *One Minute Manager* and its sequels.

Thomas G. Clark heads the real estate division of Morrison's Cafeteria, a national restaurant chain based in Atlanta. He and his wife, Marilyn, live in Dunwoody, Georgia, an Atlanta suburb, with their son, Christopher. Tom is a member of the CBMC of Norcross.

Dr. Michael Connor is director of product management for MEDSTAT Group, Inc., a health information consulting firm in Ann Arbor, Michigan, He and his wife, B. J., have a daughter, Nichole, and a son, Sean. Mike is a member of CBMC in Ann Arbor.

Victor Coppola is partner-in-charge of the emerging business group for Coopers and Lybrand in Philadelphia. He is chairman of the Delaware Valley Metro Area Council of CBMC. He and his wife, Cheryl, reside in Bryn Mawr, Pennsylvania. They have two children, Corrine and Victor, Jr.

Jack Davies is director of professional services for the Baltimore office of Right Associates. He and his wife, Caroline, live in Baltimore, Maryland, with their son, Jay, and daughter, Lynn. Jack is a member of the CBMC of Baltimore-Inner Harbor.

Dru Scott Decker is the author of *Customer Satisfaction: The Other Half of Your Job, the Telephone and Time Management*, and the Book of the Month Club feature, *How to Put More Time in Your Life*. She heads Dru Scott Associates in San Francisco and works with a number of organizations, including DuPont, AT&T, and the International Franchise Association. Her husband, Bert Decker, heads a communications consulting firm.

Phil Downer is president of the Christian Business Men's Committee of USA, based in Chattanooga, Tennessee. He, his wife, Susy, and six children, Abigail, Paul, Matthew, Joshua, Anna, and Susanna, reside in Signal Mountain, Tennessee. Before becoming part of the full-time CBMC ministry staff, he was a managing partner of an Atlanta-based law firm.

Susy Downer, her husband, Phil, and their six children reside in Signal Mountain, Tennessee. Now a full-time homemaker, she formerly served as a corporate executive and chief legal counsel for Delta Airlines.

John E. Endlich is director of the financial auditing division in the Office of the Inspector General of the U.S. Department of Energy. He and his wife, Marsha, reside in Vienna, Virginia. They have one daughter, Kelly, and a son, J. B. John is a member of CBMC in the Washington, D.C. area.

Steven Farrar is president of Point Man Leadership Ministries in Dallas, Texas. A popular conference speaker and author, his books include the best-selling *Point Man, If I'm Not Tarzan and My Wife's Not Jane, What Are We Doing in the Jungle?*, and his newest book, *Standing Tall*. Steve and his wife, Mary, have three children, Rachel, John, and Joshua.

Steve Garrison and wife, Joy, live in Santa Ana, California. They have three children, Stephanie, Mitch, and Amy, and one grandchild. Steve is a member of the CBMC of Santa Ana and has served on the CBMC of USA Board of Directors.

Rick Griffith is vice president of operations of Corporate Solutions Group, Ltd., a computer consulting and systems integration firm. He and his wife, Allison, reside in Edmond, Oklahoma, with their four children, Jenna, Lindsay, Jessie, and Lauren. Rick is a member of the CBMC of Oklahoma City-Downtown.

Clyde Hawkins passed away in 1993. He was president of Service-Master Associates, Inc., a forty-franchise distributor of services and products in Tennessee for the ServiceMaster Company. He was also a longtime member of CBMC and a former member of the CBMC national board of directors. His widow, Birdie, resides in Powell, Tennessee. They have five children, Rick, Dan, Alan, Jill, and Eric, and five grandchildren.

James S. Hewett formerly was senior pastor of Saratoga Presbyterian Church in Saratoga, California. He is editor of *Illustrations Unlimited*, a topical collection of quotes and stories for speakers, writers, pastors, and teachers. He also edits and publishes *Parables, Etc.* and *The Pastor's Story File*, two monthly newsletters of illustrations.

Bea Hicks and her husband Charles, own Hicks Insurance Service, Inc. in Rossville, Georgia. They have two children, Janet and Gary, and four grandchildren. Bea and Charles have been involved in CBMC in Chattanooga, Tennessee, for many years.

Jonathan Holljes is a financial consultant with Paul Revere Life Insurance Company in Richmond, Virginia. He and his wife, Jenifer, have two children, Sarah and Phillip. Jonathan is a member of CBMC in the Richmond area.

Hugh B. Jacks is the retired president and chief executive officer of BellSouth Services in Birmingham, Alabama. He currently is president of Potential Enterprises and Adventure Safaris. A member of the Christian Business Men's Committee in Birmingham, Hugh and his wife, Janet, have one daughter, Vicki, and one grandson, Josh.

F. David Jenkins is a financial planner with IDS Financial Services. Dave and his wife, Barbara, live in Federal Way, Washington, a Seattle suburb. They have two sons, Doug and Patrick, and two granddaughters. Active in CBMC since 1984, he is a member of the committee in Federal Way.

Skip Johnson is executive vice-president with Provident Bankshares Corporation in Baltimore, Maryland, and group manager-administration for Provident Bank of Maryland. He and his wife, Rosemary, have three daughters, Michelle, Rachel, and Danielle. Skip is a member of the CBMC Baltimore-Inner Harbor and serves as a chairman for CBMC in downtown Baltimore.

Dale Jones is executive director of Quest Atlanta '96. Before assuming that position, he was in banking for six years and served two years as development officer for Morehouse College. He is a member of the CBMC of Peachtree Center in Atlanta. Dale and his wife, Yolanda, have one son, Jordan.

Fred E. Kilgore is an attorney in York, Pennsylvania. He and his wife, Paula, have three daughters, Kathleen, Sasha, and Deborah. He is a member of CBMC in York.

Jeff Kobunski is a sales representative for Ryland Homes in Columbus, Ohio. He and his wife, Karen, reside in Granville, Ohio, with their son, Andrew. Jeff is a member of CBMC in Columbus.

Millard N. MacAdam is managing partner of Pro Active Leadership Consulting and Training in Newport Beach, California. He is also a professional speaker and a member of the CBMC of Newport Beach. He and his wife, Barbara, have two daughters, Debbie and Cindy, and a son, Scott, and six grandchildren.

Pat MacMillan is a business consultant and president of Team Resources, Inc., in Atlanta, Georgia. He is the author of *Hiring Excellence*. Pat and his wife, Jill, have two daughters, Jennifer and Becky, and a son, Matthew.

Michael L. Marker is a real estate developer in Cincinnati, Ohio. He and his wife, Carol, have two daughters, Lisa and Laura. Mike is a member of the CBMC National Board of Directors.

Jim and Louise Mathis reside in Overland Park, Kansas. They participate in many CBMC activities together as a couple. Jim's official responsibility with CBMC includes serving as chairman of the CBMC of College Boulevard in Overland Park, and as a volunteer Ministry Associate representative for CBMC in the Kansas City area.

Henry J. Miltenberger Jr., is president of Gilsbar, Inc., insurance consultants and administrators in Covington, Louisiana. He is a member of the CBMC of Covington and a member of the CBMC National Board of Directors. He and his wife, Cheryl, have one daughter, Catherine.

Jerry Molnar is owner of Molnar Personnel Agency, which specializes in the securities and commodities industry on Wall Street. He and his wife, Camy, have two daughters, Robin and Renee. A member of the CBMC of New York City-Downtown, he also is an avid surf fisherman.

Patrick O'Neal, his wife, Tina, and two children, Reilly and Casey, reside in Durham, North Carolina. As a member of the CBMC of Durham, he is helping to start two new groups in the Research Triangle Park and in nearby Chapel Hill.

William F. Osl Jr., is vice-president and division executive of information management services for AT&T. He serves more than eight thousand staff personnel in twenty-two countries. Bill has been with AT&T for more than twenty-three years, now working out of its Warren, New Jersey, center. He resides in Scotch Plains with his wife, Stephanie, and their five children, Christopher, Stephanie, Robyn, Jessica, and Emily.

Luis Palau, president of the Luis Palau Evangelistic Association in Portland, Oregon, is a world- renowned evangelist who has preached to more than ten million people in sixty countries. He also is the author of thirty-two books and booklets, including *Say Yes! How to Renew Your Spiritual Passion* (Multnomah Press).

Fred Prinzing is professor of preaching and pastoral ministries at Bethel Seminary in St. Paul, Minnesota.

Kevin Ring is a real estate developer in Walnut Creek, California. He and his wife, Gail, have four children, Christopher, Brian, Robby, and Julia. Kevin is a CBMC leader in the Walnut Creek/Concord area.

Bob Shank is senior pastor of South Coast Community Church in Irvine, California, and is president of Priority Living, a ministry to business and professional people, based in Tustin, California. A member of CBMC of Santa Ana, California, Shank is the author of the book, *Total Life Management.* Bob and his wife, Cheri, have two daughters, Shannon and Erin, and reside in Santa Ana, California.

Gary Smalley is president/founder of Today's Family, which is headquartered in Branson, Missouri. His books include *If Only He Knew, For Better or For Worse, Home Remedies,* and *The Key to Your Child's Heart.* He and his wife, Norma, have three children, Kari, Greg, and Michael.

Curt Smith is communications director and state director for U.S. Senator Dan Coats of Indiana. He is a member of the CBMC of College Park, Indiana, an Indianapolis suburb. Curt and his wife, Debbie, have four children, Stephen, Julie, Andrew, and Kimberly.

Ted Sprague is CEO of Universal Trade Shows and Conventions in Dallas, Texas, and president of Universal Sprague & Assoc. Consulting, working in the convention and tourism industry worldwide. He has served on the CBMC National Board of Directors. Ted and his wife, Tudi, have two daughters, Trisha and Trinda.

David Stoddard is the national director of Evangelism and Discipleship Development for CBMC of USA. He is responsible for maximizing the use of CBMC's "Living Proof" small group training series on lifestyle evangelism and personal discipleship. He and his wife, Anne, live in Mableton, Georgia, an Atlanta suburb, with their three children, Paul, Aaron, and Sarah.

Dr. Richard Swenson and his family reside in Menomonie, Wisconsin. He serves part-time on the medical faculty at the University of Wisconsin Medical School. He is the author of *Margin: How to Create the Emotional, Physical, Financial, and Time Reserves You Need.*

Robert J. Tamasy is National Director of Publications for the Christian Business Men's Committee of USA in Chattanooga, Tennessee. He is editor of CBMC's magazine, *CONTACT Quarterly,* and co-author of several books. Bob and his wife, Sally, have three daughters, Amy, Rebecca, and Sarah, and reside in Hixson, Tennessee.

Dr. William Terry is a retired urologist in Cape Girardeau, Missouri. He is a member of the CBMC of USA National Board of Directors and a leader of the CBMC ministry in Cape Girardeau. Bill and his wife, Eloise, have four children, Carolyn, Alan, Susan, and David, and ten grandchildren.

John Trent is president of Encouraging Word and presents seminars on "The Blessing" across the United States. He is an author and has written a number of books with Gary Smalley. He and his wife, Cynthia, have two daughters, Kari Lorraine and Laura Catherine.

Robert Vernon is the author of *L.A. Justice: Lessons from the Firestorm*, published by Focus on the Family. A member of the Christian Business Men's Committee, he also serves on the national board of the Fellowship of Christian Peace Officers. Robert and his wife, Esther, have one daughter, Pam, and a son, Bob, and live in Pasadena, California.

Randal Walti describes himself as "CEO Coach" with his company, Oaktree Consulting Group in Torrance, California. He is member of the CBMC Palos Verdes and chairman of the CBMC Southern California Leadership Council. Randal and his wife, Judi, have three grown children, Lee, Rod, and Lynn, and four grandchildren.

Chip Weiant is executive vice-president for Schmidt's Hospitality Companies, a Columbus, Ohio-based national restaurant and food brand management corporation. He and his wife, Anne, live in Columbus with their three children, Kate, Leslie, and Sam. Chip is a member of CBMC in Columbus.

Mary Whelchel is head of her own business training company, Whelchel and Associates, specializing in sales, telemarketing, and customer service. She is the author of *The Christian Working Woman* and *Common Mistakes Singles Make*. Mary has one daughter, Julie Busteed.

David R. Willcox is a founding partner of SENERGEN and president of Human Resources Management, Inc., organizational consulting firms that specialize in group effectiveness and team building. He and his wife, Janet, live in Glen Ridge, New Jersey. They have four children and three grandchildren. Dave is a member of CBMC in Newark, New Jersey.

Alexander S. Williams is executive vice-president of First Fidelty Bank in Newark, New Jersey. A former mayor of Westfield, New Jersey, he and his wife, Jennie, reside in Westfield. They have a daughter, Toni Winslow; a son, Billy; and two grandchildren. Alex is a member of the CBMC of Newark.